INTERNATIONAL DIMENSIONS OF ACCOUNTING

The Kent International Business Series

DAVID A. RICKS
Series Consulting Editor

KENT PUBLISHING COMPANY
A Division of Wadsworth, Inc.
Boston, Massachusetts

INTERNATIONAL DIMENSIONS OF ACCOUNTING

Jeffrey S. Arpan
University of South Carolina

Dhia D. AlHashim
California State University, Northridge

This book is dedicated
to Kathy and Shatha

Editor: John B. McHugh
Production Editor: Michael Paladini
Cover and Text Designer: Armen Kojoyian
Production Coordinator: Linda Siegrist

Kent Publishing Company
A Division of Wadsworth, Inc.

Printed in the United States of America
1 2 3 4 5 6 7 8 9—87 86 85 84 83

Library of Congress Cataloging in Publication Data

Arpan, Jeffrey S.
The international dimensions of accounting.

(The International dimensions of business)
Includes bibliographical references and index.
1. International business enterprises—Accounting.
2. Accounting. I. AlHashim, Dhia D. II. Title.
III. Series.
HF5686.I56A77 1983 657'.95 83-18747
ISBN 0-534-01467-4

Series Foreword

Prior to World War II, the number of firms involved in foreign direct investment was relatively small. Although several U.S. companies were obtaining raw materials from other countries, most firms were only interested in the U.S. market. This changed, however, during the 1950s—especially after the creation of the European Economic Community. Since that time, there has been a rapid expansion in international business activity.

The majority of the world's large corporations now perform an increasing proportion of their business activities outside of their home country. For many of these companies, international business returns over one-half of their profits, and it is becoming more and more common for a typical corporation to earn at least one-fourth of its profits through international business involvement. In fact, it is now rather rare for any large firm not to be a participant in the world of international business.

International business is of great importance in most countries and that importance continues to grow. To meet the demand for increased knowledge in this area, business schools are attempting to add international dimensions to their curricula. Faculty members are becoming more interested in teaching a greater variety of international business courses and are striving to add international dimensions to other courses. Students, aware of the increasing probability that they will be employed by firms engaged in international business activities, are seeking knowledge of the problem-solving techniques unique to international business. As the American Assembly of Collegiate Schools of Business has observed, however, there is a shortage of information available. Most business textbooks do not adequately consider the international dimensions of business and much of the supplemental material is disjointed, overly narrow or otherwise inadequate in the classroom.

This series has been developed to overcome such problems. The books are written by some of the most respected authors in the various areas of international business. Each author is extremely well known in the Academy of International Business and in his other professional academies. Each possesses an outstanding knowledge of his subject matter and a talent for explaining it.

These books, in which the authors have identified the most important international aspects of their fields, have been written in a format which facilitates their use as supplemental material in business school courses. For the most part, the material is presented by topic in approximately the same order and manner as it is covered in basic business textbooks. Therefore, as each topic is covered in the course, material is easily supplemented with the corresponding chapter in the series book.

The Kent Series in International Business offers a unique and much needed opportunity to bring international dimensions of business into the classroom. The series has been developed by leaders in the field after years of discussion and careful consideration, and the timely encouragement and support provided by Keith Nave, Kent Senior Editor on this project. I am proud to be associated with this series and highly recommend it to you.

David A. Ricks

Consulting Editor to the Kent Series in International Business
Professor of International Business, University of South Carolina

Preface

Although Wendell Willkie many decades ago spoke euphemistically about "one world," really only within the last ten years has the true meaning of "one world" become economically clear for most people. In the U.S., no home seems complete without a Japanese television, clothing from France or Hong Kong, or an imported car. Similarly, consumers in other countries drink Coca Cola, have G.E. kitchen appliances, wear Levi's jeans, and eat Kentucky Fried Chicken. The same sort of economic internationalization has occurred throughout the world's business communities. Foreign firms use U.S.-made computers, American auto firms use foreign-made components, and nearly every country uses Middle Eastern oil. In addition, U.S. firms have investments in other countries, and vice versa.

Increasing international trade of products, services, technology, and expertise, as well as increasing foreign investment, both in and by foreign countries, have been the driving forces of internationalization. Behind the expansion of international business there is the common desire in countries to upgrade their standards of living, even as they face domestic shortages of the means to do so. In short, similar aspirations but different capabilities have resulted in an increasingly interwoven world, even in spite of several strong feelings, such as intense nationalism, that would impede the process.

No matter what its cause or desirability, the rapid expansion of international business activity has led to new problems and challenges for the accounting, business, and financial communities. These problems include, first, simply doing business internationally, and, second, providing information and services to firms that do, and to those people who invest in, loan money to, or otherwise interact with firms operating internationally.

In fact, the common denominator of the problems associated with doing business internationally is the proper generation and interpretation of internationally related information. Old methods of accounting and financial analysis are no longer adequate. Flows of goods, services, and capital across national borders have generated the "international" dimensions of accounting. That is, accounting procedures and analysis have been forced to take into account new types of transactions, events, and relationships hitherto largely ignored, such as the changes in the exchange value of a currency and their impact on corporate earnings. Without such adaptations and modifications, users of accounting information could be easily misled without knowing it, and hence, they would not make the proper decisions.

The purpose of this book is to identify and explain several major aspects of accounting's international dimensions. It is intended as a supplementary text for undergraduate and graduate courses in accounting, and as a text for professional accountants and financial executives as well. It cannot and does not cover *all* aspects of international accounting. Rather, more than anything else, this text seeks to increase the reader's awareness, and to extend his or her horizons beyond purely domestic accounting.

ORGANIZATION AND USE OF THE TEXT

These pages encompass the major international dimensions of financial accounting, managerial accounting, and auditing, and also include information about the accounting profession in various countries. Because few accounting courses cover all of these four areas, certain chapters of *International Dimensions of Accounting* will not be appropriate for some classes. In addition, this book assumes that the reader is already familiar with domestic accounting principles and procedures. Therefore, *International Dimensions of Accounting* is best suited for use after specific domestic situations have been covered.

Chapter 1 provides an overview of the need for international skills, an explanation of why accounting and accountants are different in different countries, and a discussion of some of the special problems that these differences pose for multinational enterprises.

Chapter 2 covers the methods by which accounting standards are established in various countries, and why particular methods are chosen or necessitated. The specific countries discussed are Brazil, France, Germany, Japan, the Netherlands, Switzerland, the United Kingdom, and the United States. The chapter also describes the progress of efforts to lessen differences in accounting practices around the world.

Chapter 3 provides a general discussion of the difficulties encountered in analyzing foreign financial statements, and focuses on both the differences of valuation and income determination procedures and cosmetic differences of style and format. It also highlights the shortcomings of using the techniques of financial analysis developed in one country on the financial statements from another country.

Chapter 4 continues the general subject of valuation and income determination begun in Chapter 3. However, its focus is entirely on inflation accounting—a subject too lengthy to cover adequately as part of Chapter 3. Chapter 4 covers the basic theoretical approaches to inflation accounting as well as describing the specific approaches taken in Germany, France, Chile, the Netherlands, Brazil, and the United Kingdom (with comparisons to the United States).

Chapters 5, 6, and 7 contain material more directly related to the operational accounting aspects of multinational firms. Chapter 5 deals with several major financial reporting issues, such as consolidation, foreign exchange gains and losses due to transactions and translation, segment reporting, and social accounting. Chapter 6 covers the major international aspects of managerial accounting, such as planning and budgeting, investment analysis, product costing, performance evaluation, and control processes. Finally, Chapter 7 covers the international aspects of auditing, both internal and external, including the accounting implications of the Foreign Corrupt Practices Act and a description of the activities of international public accounting firms. It also contains some information about the auditing profession and its standards in several countries.

ACKNOWLEDGEMENTS

We are grateful for all those pioneers in the field of international accounting without whom interest in this field would not have materialized, and especially for the efforts of S. Paul Garner, Emeritus Dean of the University of Alabama, Vernon K. Zimmerman of the University of Illinois, and Gerhard G. Mueller of the University of Washington.

The authors acknowledge the constructive comments of the reviewers of the manuscript of this text, Professor Irving L. Fantl of Florida International University, and Professor Lee H. Radebaugh of Brigham Young University. We also wish to thank Michael Paladini for his skillful copyediting of the manuscript.

Finally, we assume responsibility for whatever weaknesses may be present in *International Dimensions of Accounting*. Readers' comments on this text would be gratefully appreciated.

Jeffrey S. Arpan — Columbia, South Carolina
Dhia D. AlHashim — Northridge, California
1983

Contents

INTERNATIONAL DIMENSIONS OF ACCOUNTING

Chapter 1

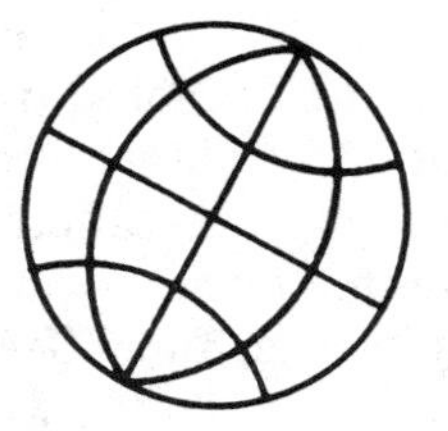

Introduction and Overview

Due to the explosive growth of international business over the last two decades, increasing attention necessarily has been paid to the international problems of accounting. A few statistics provide an indication of the magnitude of recent international business transactions. During the last two decades, the direct investment of U.S. companies abroad more than tripled, increasing from about \$52 billion in 1966 to over \$170 billion in 1979. In the other direction, the increase was even more marked. The direct investment of foreign-based companies in the U.S. increased from \$9 billion in 1966 to about \$41 billion in 1978. In 1979 alone, the value of new direct investment by foreign investors in the U.S. increased by more than \$15 billion, and in 1980, by approximately \$10 billion, to a level of nearly \$70 billion. Most of these investments were made by companies based in the United Kingdom, the Netherlands, Germany, and Canada, and about 20% of these investments in the U.S. were made by developing nations. In addition, based on the latest estimate of the Arab Federation of Chambers of Trade, Industry, and Agriculture, the total foreign investment by the Arab oil-producing countries has now reached approximately \$405 billion, and this figure is expected to rise to \$990 billion by 1985.

Furthermore, the total value of international trade for the U.S. in 1981 was approximately half a trillion dollars, exports totalling \$235 billion and imports about $262 billion. For most European and newly industrialized countries, international trade accounts for a significant share (usually more than 25%) of their economic activity. Finally, more than 50% of the income of many international corporations over the last few years was generated from operations outside their native countries (for example, IBM, Nestlé, and CIBA–GEIGY). In short, the economies of virtually every country in the world have become increasingly interconnected by international business developments and activities.

Yet the impact of international developments affects far more than just the firms engaged in international business. As the OPEC oil embargo and price hikes of the 1970s clearly demonstrated, even purely domestic firms in most countries felt the impact of international developments through oil shortages, higher energy prices, and the resulting economic recessions. In addition, many domestic firms closed and workers were unemployed due to increased competition in domestic markets from imports.

As a result of these international business developments, the professional accounting, business, and financial communities had to pay greater attention to international business activities and the international problems of accounting. As international business competition increased, new challenges arose (both threats and opportunities). Firms' failures to understand and anticipate these challenges increasingly led to decreased international competitiveness and financial performance, and in some cases, bankruptcy. Many of the firms that attempted to expand internationally found the international aspects of business difficult. Managers often found that proven ways of doing business successfully in their domestic markets were not always successful in foreign countries. Competitive conditions were unfamiliar, different laws were involved, and business and cultural practices varied from country to country—including accounting standards and practices. In addition, many firms confronted, for the first time, dealing in foreign currencies and the ensuing problems of foreign exchange gains and losses. In the meantime, firms facing import competition lacked knowledge of what supported the foreign exporters' success; as a result, these domestic firms did not know how to compete with foreign firms or how to diminish their competitive impact.

In short, firms in virtually all countries were suddenly confronted with the need to increase their international awareness and skills, and yet only a small percentage of them had the existing capability to do so. Perhaps ironically, of all industrialized nations, the shortage of international capability was most acute in the United States, where a large domestic market had for so long insulated U.S. firms from international activities. In addition, domestic investors and creditors found it increasingly difficult to understand the financial reports of firms with international activities. The investors and creditors, too, lacked an adequate understanding of the international aspects of business, and so the internationalized financial statements being prepared by firms often seemed confusing to them.

In response to the new need for international awareness and skills in the U.S. business and financial communities, new educational programs had to be developed. For example, the American Assembly of Collegiate Schools of Business (AACSB) changed its accreditation standards in 1974 to include a requirement that the international dimensions of business be added to the undergraduate and graduate curricula.

The American Accounting Association also recognized that future accountants should be knowledgeable about the international dimension of business, and particularly about the international aspects of accounting. It formally recognized this need in 1978, by calling for significant increases in the international content of the accounting curriculum. The reasons for this change are clear. Accounting reports prepared on the bases of different national accounting standards and kept in many different national languages and currencies need to be adjusted, translated and consolidated. These reports must be prepared to satisfy the needs of owners, various governments, and international agencies.

The flow of accounting reports across national borders generates the real need for an international dimension in accounting. Accounting is the language of business. For it to serve the needs of international investors, creditors, and managers, it must become an international language that seeks to harmonize accounting standards and reports.

But apart from the needs of international investors, creditors, and managers, there is another important reason for studying international accounting: to learn from the experiences of other countries. While accounting can serve many different purposes, it also serves similar purposes in many countries. Yet, at the same time, while the purposes may be the same in different countries, there are often differences in the approach taken. Accounting for inflation is a good example. Almost all countries attempt to account for inflation, but their approaches differ. Some methods of accounting for inflation are more successful than others. By studying how various countries account for inflation, and what successes they have, another country can more efficiently design or adapt its own approach. The same general benefits can be gleaned from the study of many other foreign accounting practices. Finally, studying another country's accounting system also helps the individual to understand better his or her own country's accounting system.

The objectives of this chapter are to explain the variety of accounting practices and practitioners throughout the world, and to identify the need both for a better understanding of the international dimensions of accounting and for a greater similarity of accounting systems and professions among nations.

ENVIRONMENTAL INFLUENCES ON ACCOUNTING

The most general purpose of accounting is to provide financial information to people for decision-making purposes. Therefore, one of the major reasons accounting is done differently in various countries is because the users and preparers of accounting information are themselves different. For example, people differ in their educational backgrounds, which determine the sophistication of information they can absorb and understand. In the extreme case, if they cannot read, they cannot make use of written financial reports. In less extreme cases, if they are unable to understand consolidation procedures, they will not make effective use of consolidated financial statements. Or, if they lack familiarity with the meaning of earnings per share, then they cannot make use of that kind of information. Therefore, the sophistication and complexity of accounting varies directly with the sophistication and education of the users of accounting information. It also varies directly with the sophistication and education of the people who prepare the statements: the accountants. If the accountants are not sophisticated enough to understand how to account for foreign exchange gains and losses, or even for inflation, then the accounting procedures for these phenomena will not be developed or utilized correctly. As this chapter and Chapter 7 describe, the educational backgrounds and expertise of accountants in foreign countries vary widely.

Users also differ in the information they want from financial reports. Creditors want one kind of information, investors want other kinds of information, governments have still other needs, while employees want information that may not be important to the other three. Because accounting seeks to provide the information desired by its users, accounting grows more complicated as there are more varieties of users and as the kinds of information they require become more varied. In societies where the government owns all enterprises, and where the desire of the government is to use accounting information primarily for national economic planning and decision-making purposes, a single, highly standardized and uniform system of accounting typically develops. In countries where most industrial enterprises are privately owned by a small number of very wealthy families, accounting reports are not likely to be numerous or publicly available. Where business operations rely heavily on bank credit, accounting is likely to be creditor-oriented rather than investor-oriented. These situations differ sharply from the conditions found in the United States, which has a large investing public, thousands of publicly held firms, a highly organized stock market with a strong regulatory agency, the Securities and Exchange Commission, and virtually no government ownership of, or government economic planning for, business enterprises. As a result, U.S. accounting reports tend to be more varied and investor-oriented. In short, the more users of information there are in a country, and the greater the differences among the needs of those users, the more complex a country's accounting procedures and reports are likely to be.

However, differences in accounting uses, users, and preparers form only one dimension of the many environmental factors that influence accounting. Sociocultural, legal and political, and economic conditions also have an impact upon a country's accounting standards and practices.

Sociocultural Conditions

Among the major and more interesting sociocultural conditions that influence accounting are a people's attitude toward secrecy, time, fate, and business.

The attitude toward secrecy in a country largely influences the collection and dissemination of accounting information, and is generally related to the degree of trust people have in each other and in their institutions. Logically, in a country where people are generally secretive, they are not likely to provide much information to others, whether in accounting or in any other field. It is difficult in such a country to obtain accounting information from businesses, and what can be obtained is usually not very detailed. Therefore, external reports are seldom prepared and are not very well disclosed, and auditing is difficult.

We should add that this is generally true unless the country either has a strong government agency to enforce public disclosure (such as the Securities Exchange Commission) or the individual firm sees some benefit from publicly disclosing financial information. Curiously, a high degree of trust may also result in low levels of external reporting and disclosure, simply *because* everyone trusts each other. In such cases, there may be little perceived need to require written verification of a firm's financial position or the results of its operations.

How people regard time also shapes accounting practices. In countries where people have a longer view of time and a diminished sense of urgency, the balance sheet is likely to be given more importance than the income statement, and financial reports are likely to be published less frequently. This situation is widely prevalent in most developing countries, but one also finds evidence of a more relaxed attitude about time, although to a lesser degree, in some developed countries, such as Japan, Germany, and Switzerland. In such situations, income determination is not viewed as important. In the United States, however, the orientation is more short-term; that is, there is a higher sense of urgency in the society and, hence, more emphasis on the income statement and, in fact, quarterly income statements! Consequently, as will be discussed in Chapter 3, valuation and other accounting principles related to income determination are more developed and important in the United States than in many other nations.

A people's attitude towards fate also affects accounting, particularly certain aspects of managerial accounting. If the dominant belief is that there is no control over events or life in general, then there is little perceived need for planning, budgeting, performance evaluation, or other means of control. Hence, there is also little perceived need for accounting policies and procedures related to planning and control. After all, why prepare forecasts of funds flows when nothing can be done to alter what will actually happen? Or why prepare variance analyses after the fact when nothing could have been done to prevent what happened from happening? In short, the more fatalistic a country, the lower its development of managerial accounting is likely to be.

Finally, the prevailing attitude towards business as a whole has several influences on accounting—most notably, the degree of public disclosure and the amount of social responsibility accounting. A negative or distrustful attitude towards business will be likely to result in legislation that requires greater disclosure in, and greater reliability or verifiability of, financial statements (as is the case in the United States and the United Kingdom). Regarding what is reported, in countries where people believe that a firm has a purpose in and a responsbility towards society much larger than merely earning profits and financial returns for stockholders, there is likely to be additional information concerning these wider responsibilities contained in corporate financial reports or in specially prepared reports. Social responsibility accounting is particularly developed and prevalent in socialist countries, but it is rapidly emerging in Continental Europe as well.

Legal and Political Conditions

In most countries of the world, government has a very direct impact on accounting practices: the government determines and enforces them. It does so by legislating or simply dictating what accounting procedures must be followed. In many countries, this practice takes place because the professional accounting body is not strong enough, or no professional accounting body exists capable of developing suitable or needed accounting procedures. In other countries, accounting procedures are legislated because all business practices are legislated, or because the enterprises are owned, regulated, or directed by the government. And in virtually all countries, some government-determined accounting procedures exist for the purposes of taxation.

Because the government is itself a user of accounting information, the same phenomena occur and conclusions apply concerning the relationship between the users of accounting information and accounting itself that were discussed earlier in this chapter. For example, the U.S. government requires accounting information for taxation and a host of regulatory purposes, such as occupational safety and health, environmental protection, the enforcement of antitrust laws, and so on. Yet because it does not plan or direct private sector economic activity, it hardly legislates or collects the type of accounting information that the Soviet Union does. On the other hand, the government of Chad does not have much of a business sector to regulate, direct, or tax, so its accounting regulations are not terribly complicated, to put it mildly. In this range can be found many emerging nations, such as Brazil and Egypt, where the government takes an active role in industrial development of leading economic sectors, but lets small-scale economic activity largely operate on its own. Such countries' governments tend to develop fairly complex accounting procedures for its large firms, while allowing small businesses to operate under altogether different procedures.

Governmental stability also influences accounting in a number of ways. In countries where accounting rules are set by the government and where major changes in the parties or individuals governing the country are frequent, accounting procedures undergo similar changes. For example, the recent social accounting trend in France reflects the growing socialist power in French government. Another example is the major change in Egyptian accounting procedures which occurred when Nasser nationalized most of the Egyptian economy during the 1960s. Naturally, governmental instability also tends to result in economic instability. Economic instability, in turn, puts certain demands on accounting, such as accounting for inflation, changes in exchange rates, and so forth. Under such conditions, accounting conservatism increases due to the general uncertainty about future economic and political trends.

Economic Conditions

Perhaps the greatest of all environmental characteristics that influence accounting is a nation's economic condition. Fundamentally, the complexity of the economy is directly related to accounting complexity. That is, an agrarian, subsistence-type economy requires only a rudimentary accounting system, but as industrialization occurs, a more advanced accounting system is needed. For example, accounting for fixed assets becomes more important, and numerous new forms of enterprise organization (partnerships, corporations, and so on) require the development of new accounting procedures. As an economy becomes more complex, so too do the types of economic transactions, such as credit sales, leases, mergers, and acquisitions, complexities that also require more complex accounting procedures. Public sector accounting and tax accounting also assume greater importance as the size of the public sector grows, along with its financial needs.

In an economically complex society, international business activity assumes more importance. As international trade expands, countries begin to worry about balance of payments and foreign exchange. Thus, governments must develop accounting systems to monitor trade flows, to observe foreign currency stocks and their flows, to assess import duties, and so on. For the domestic firms involved in international trade, new accounting procedures are needed to assess gains and losses due to changes in the value of currencies—a subject described in greater detail in Chapter 5.

Finally, in countries that are economically unstable, inflation becomes another influence on accounting procedures and practices. Of course, if a country has never experienced inflation, it is not likely to have developed extensive inflation accounting procedures. Countries that have experienced persistent hyperinflation (triple-digit inflation) usually develop a thoroughgoing inflation accounting system. And, as we pointed out earlier, economic instability in general tends to result in more conservative accounting practices, such as the significant use of reserves, major allowances for bad debts, and rapid depreciation rates.

The Need for Environmental Analysis

It should be clear by now that a country's environmental characteristics determine the needs and various uses for accounting, and specific accounting policies, procedures, and practices. Therefore, to understand properly any country's accounting system one must understand the country's environment. This is true even for properly understanding the accounting system of one's own country. Otherwise, accounting information simply will not be correctly prepared, analyzed, or used. We elaborate on this considerably in Chapter 3 in terms of conducting financial analysis. However, the need for environmental analysis is also a recurrent theme throughout this book, and in the daily lives of accountants working for international enterprises.

THE ACCOUNTING PROFESSION WORLDWIDE

From our discussion of the environmental influences on accounting systems and procedures, one could correctly assume that environmental factors also influence the accounting profession itself: the kinds of people who aspire to become accountants, the status and remuneration of accountants, and the skills required to be an accountant. The higher the income and social status of accountants, the more people will aspire to careers in accounting. And in most cases, the higher the status of accountants, the higher will be the qualifications for becoming an accountant, and vice versa. In addition, the more complex the accounting system needs to be, due to the complexity and development of a nation's economy, the higher the skills of that nation's accountants will need to be. Thus, an "accountant" in one country is not necessarily the same as an "accountant" in another country.

In most countries of the world, there are at least two major types of accountants: those who are "certified" by some formal process, and those who are not "certified." Certain accounting activities can be performed only by certified accountants, such as performing external audits in the United States. Other accounting activities, such as preparing an individual's tax return or working in the accounting department of a firm can be performed by noncertified accountants. The major differences within the accounting profession throughout the world surround the certified variety of accountants. We will now turn our attention to these differences as they appear in a few selected countries, beginning with a summary of the U.S. certification process to serve as a frame of reference for discussing other countries.

The United States

In the United States, to follow the licensing system for entry into the public accounting profession is to become a "Certified Public Accountant" (CPA). The licensing is done by each individual state, and so it varies from one state to another. In general, though, to become a CPA requires a specified number of hours of education in accounting (typically at a university), an "experience" requirement, and passing a rigorous comprehensive examination administered by the American Institute of Certified Public Accountants, the professional organization of practicing CPAs. The examination covers business law, accounting theory, accounting practice, and auditing. At least two parts must be passed simultaneously to obtain credit for any part of the exam, resulting in a "conditional pass." The remaining parts must then be passed within a specified period of time. Failure to pass at least two parts requires the candidate to retake the entire exam. Due to the comparatively lengthy and stringent standards for becoming a CPA in the United States, American CPAs enjoy a "professional status," and are generally well remunerated for the services they render. There are approximately 200,000 CPAs in the United States.

West Germany

The German equivalent of an American CPA is a *Wirtschaftsprüfer*. To become a *Wirtschaftsprüfer*, a person must graduate from a university in law, economics, and business, and gain five years of practical experience in a business, including at least four years in the accounting profession. Then, the person must pass both a written and an oral examination on accounting and business matters, commercial and tax law, accounting practices, and professional ethics. Due to the stringent membership and qualification requirements in Germany, German "CPAs" enjoy a high social status, but there are fewer than 4,000 of them and few candidates qualify before the age of 32.

France

The status of the French accounting profession has improved significantly in the past two decades. The profession is regulated by the French government under legislation first enacted in 1945. Specific government control of the profession rests with the Order of Accounting Experts (*L'Ordre des Experts Comptables et des Comptables Agréés*) in which membership is compulsory. Public accounting services in France must be offered *only* by members of the Order, or by organizations controlled by such members.

In France, two distinct categories of accountants are legally recognized: the *expert comptable* and the *comptable agréé*. The former is the equivalent of CPA in the U.S., while the latter functions mainly as a public bookkeeper. To become a member of the Order of Accounting Experts, each category faces different requirements.

For an *expert comptable*, a candidate must pass three examinations. A preliminary exam is intended to determine the candidate's aptitude for continuing with a higher technical education. The second examination covers accounting, economics, and law, and, if passed, results in the conferring of the *Diplôme d'Etudes Comptables Superior* (DECS).

Before taking the third examination, a candidate must complete a minimum of three years' training, either as an apprentice to an *expert comptable* or as an official of the Ministry of the Economy. The final exam consists of a compulsory portion, covering auditing, financial management, and company law, and an elective portion, where the candidate chooses to be examined on one of four subjects: law, data processing, the Common Market and international economics, or management organization and control. Finally, the "survivors" must successfully submit and defend an original thesis on a professional subject.

The qualifications for a *comptable agréé* are less demanding. The person must hold a *DECS* and have had two years practical experience to qualify.

Italy

In Italy, there are two categories of recognized professional accountants: the Doctor of Commerce (*Dottore Commercialista*) and the Accountant and Commercial Expert (*Ragioniere e Perito Commerciale*). However, despite the fact that the educational requirements for becoming the latter are less than those for the former, Italian law does not distinguish between the two in the actual practice of their profession.

The *Dottore* is a university graduate who has studied economics, accounting, banking, and law, has passed oral and written examinations, and has completed a thesis on an approved subject. Thereafter, the candidate must pass a state-controlled examination in order to join the professional body, the Order of Doctors of Commerce. Unlike Germany, however, no practical professional experience is required before taking the state examination. Also unlike Germany, the Order of Doctors of Commerce has not published any official code of ethics or any recommendations on accounting principles or audit practices. There are currently over 15,000 *Dottori*, about half being in public service.

To become a *Ragioniere*, a person must obtain a diploma from a business school where the course of study includes accounting, mathematics, and law; then the individual must pass a state controlled examination. However, to become a member of the Accountants Association (*Collegio dei' Ragionieri*), a person must obtain two years of practical experience in the office of a *Dottore Commercialista* or *Ragionieri* engaged in public practice, and then pass another written and oral exam on taxation, accounting matters, and the provisions of the Civil Code. There are approximately 7000 members of the *Collegio*, nearly all of whom are in public accounting.

Spain

The accounting profession in Spain is not organized in ways that would be familiar to many developed countries. It is led predominantly by the *Institute de Censores Surados de Cuentas de España*, which was organized in 1944 and is under the control of the Ministry of Commerce. Admission to the Institute is by examination, and is open to any candidate who holds a degree in economics or a similar subject, who is of Spanish nationality, and who possesses all civil rights. The Institute has attempted to require of its prospective members two years of apprenticeship and a written thesis. It also has a comprehensive code of professional ethics and conduct. However, there is no protection for the term "accountant"; that is, *anyone* can offer accounting or tax services to the public.

Colombia

In Colombia, a government agency that was formed in 1960, the Central Board of Accountancy (*Junta Central de Contadores*), approves, issues, and controls the licensing of public accountants and public accounting firms. Roughly fifty firms and 5000 accountants are currently registered with the Board. In addition, there is a National Institute of Public Accountants (*Instituto Nacional de Contadore Publicos*), which was formed in 1952 for the primary purpose of securing regulatory legislation and order in the development of the public accounting profession. Its current membership numbers around 500.

The two types of accountants specified in Law 142 (passed in 1960) are a certified public accountant, *contador publico titulado*, or *CPT*), and the authorized public accountant, *contador publico autorizado*, or *CPA*. To obtain the title *CPT*, a person must have a degree from a recognized Colombian or foreign university, and one year's experience in public or private accounting. In accordance with the laws prior to December of 1960, the title of *CPA* was obtained simply by being licensed; but as of December of 1962 the title of *CPA* is obtained by having met certain requirements and by having applied for and received registration with the Central Board. In addition, all *CPT*s and *CPA*s must be: (1) a Colombian citizen, or a citizen of another country that has reciprocity of certification who has resided in Colombia for at least three years, and who has passed examinations on the Spanish language and Colombian legislation; (2) a person with high morals; and (3) a person who has not violated the written code of professional ethics.

Japan

Japanese CPAs have had far less time to develop as a strong and respected auditing profession than their counterparts in Anglo-Saxon countries. In fact, Japan's first national law to establish a modern accounting profession was not passed until 1948. Before World War II, Japan's accounting profession was primarily influenced by European practices and company laws. Naturally, the post-war revision of its accounting profession was heavily influenced by the United States.

Three separate examinations must be passed to become a CPA (*Konin Kaikeishi*) in Japan. The first examination covers the candidate's knowledge and understanding of the field of liberal arts. (College students study liberal arts and are exempted from this preliminary exam). The second, or intermediate, examination covers seven subjects, all of which must be passed in *one* sitting: bookkeeping, accounting theory, cost accounting, auditing, business administration, economics, and commercial law. This intermediate examination is so difficult that historically the passing rate has been approximately 5%. If the candidate is successful, he can then register with the Ministry of Finance as a junior CPA (*Kaikeishi ho*)—but he still cannot certify financial statements. The final examination can be taken only after the candidate has completed an additional year of prescribed training and has two years of auditing or accounting experience. The final examination covers advanced accounting, auditing practice, financial statement analysis, tax practice, and an oral segment testing the candidate's ability to apply his knowledge to practical situations. It should come as no surprise that only about 300 Japanese become CPAs each year.

SPECIAL ACCOUNTING PROBLEMS FOR MULTINATIONAL ENTERPRISES

The difference in accounting systems throughout the world is much more than an interesting intellectual subject. It poses a constant problem and challenge for any multinational enterprise (MNE) which, by definition, operates in several countries and therefore across several accounting systems. A multinational firm must be aware of and analyze the competitive conditions in the countries where it operates in order to make best use of its scarce resources, to ward off threats, and to take advantage of opportunities. To do these things, it must be able to interpret information about any developments in its markets or in a nation's politics, information about its existing or potential competitors, and information about the success of its own global operations. Thus, the proper analysis of data coming from various parts of the world is critical for making good management decisions. The firm's accountants play a major role in this analysis.

On the external side, MNEs must also prepare reports for investors, creditors, and the governments of several countries. The reports must be prepared in a manner that is useful and acceptable to these various groups, a task which will often require restating these reports in different languages, currencies, or formats, or using different accounting procedures. Sometimes special reports must be prepared—special social accounting reports, for example—which will include information that does not generally appear in the usual reports. To conduct all these activities properly, the MNE's accounting staff is called upon to be adequately knowledgeable and trained.

To give an example of the accounting challenge that is often involved, consider the fairly simple case of a U.S. firm with a joint venture in Brazil. By Brazilian law, the official accounting records of the Brazilian operation must be denominated in cruzeiros, must be written in Portugese, and must be prepared and maintained according to Brazilian accounting procedures. In addition, the Brazilian subsidiary must report to the Brazilian government and shareholders in a method, format, and frequency dictated by Brazilian accounting law. At the same time, the North American parent company is required by U.S. tax laws to prepare a consolidated, global tax return for the U.S. government. Because of "generally accepted accounting procedures" (GAAP), the firm must prepare a consolidated global financial report to its U.S. shareholders. And, if the firm's stock is traded on the stock exchange, it must prepare a report for the SEC. The North American reports must be done in dollars, in English, and according to U.S. tax regulations and U.S. GAAP. Obviously, the accounts and numbers of the Brazilian subsidiary's books cannot be simply added to the parent firm's books without several conversions being made in currency, language, format, and accounting procedures.

The Brazlian government and shareholders may also require some information about the parent company's operations. This information must be again converted, although in this case, in the opposite direction. Then, too, for internal decision making, the parent company needs to know how its Brazilian subsidiary fares in order to be sure that it is performing as expected. Thus, the subsidiary must report frequently to the parent, and there must be some communication in the other direction as well. To expedite these internal communication flows, it is helpful to utilize common standardized procedures, including a common language, currency, and format.

In sum, there is a critical need for personnel who understand and can function in the languages, accounting systems, and cultures of both countries. Because such people are in short supply, it would be much easier for MNEs, and for anyone else who uses accounting information from another country, if the existing differences in accounting systems were eliminated. It would be nice if all countries did accounting in the same way, and if all the world's accountants had similar training. Of course, this ideal situation is far from the real situation of today. However, efforts continue to be made on several levels to lessen the differences. This process, called harmonization, is one subject of Chapter 2.

STUDY QUESTIONS FOR CHAPTER 1

1. What are the major benefits of learning about the international dimensions of accounting?
2. How can studying other countries' accounting systems help a nation evaluate and perhaps improve its own system?
3. What is the major reason why accounting systems of different nations are so different?
4. Explain how differences in levels of economic development affect the development and complexity of a nation's accounting system.
5. In what ways would a low level of literacy complicate the development of a nation's accounting system?
6. Accounting records of foreign subsidiaries are based on different accounting standards and procedures, and are in different currencies and languages. What do you think are some of the major problems a parent company faces in preparing a consolidated global report under these conditions?
7. What are some of the major differences around the world in the requirements for becoming a "certified" public accountant?
8. What causes the differences in accountant certification procedures around the world?

ADDITIONAL REFERENCES

1. AlHashim, Dhia D., and Robertson, James W. *Accounting for Multinational Enterprises*, Indianapolis, Indiana: Bobbs-Merrill Educational Publishing, 1978, Chapter 1.
2. American Accounting Association. "Report of the American Accounting Association Committee on International Accounting." *Accounting Review*, Supplement 1976.
3. Arpan, Jeffrey S., and Radebaugh, Lee H. *International Account-*

ing and Multinational Enterprises. Boston, Massachusetts: Warren, Gorham & Lamont, 1981, Chapters 1–2.

4. Bedford, Norton M., and Gautier, Jacques P. "An International Analytical Comparison of the Structure and Content of Annual Reports in the European Economic Community, Switzerland and the United States." *International Journal of Accounting,* Spring 1974.
5. Burton, John C. *The International World of Accounting: Challenges and Opportunities.* Reston, Virginia: Arthur Young & Co., 1981, Section I.
6. Choi, Frederick D. S., and Mueller, Gerhard G. *An Introduction to Multinational Accounting.* Englewood Cliffs, New Jersey: Prentice-Hall, 1978, Chapters 1–2, 4–6.
7. Deloitte Haskins & Sells. *International Accounting Standards and Guidelines.* New York: Deloitte Haskins & Sells, January 1981.
8. Enthoven, Adolf J. H. *Accountancy and Economic Development Policy.* New York: Americn Elsevier Publishing Co., 1975.
9. Fitzgerald, Richard D., Stickler, A. D., and Watts, T. R. *International Survey of Accounting Principles and Reporting Practices.* New York: Price Waterhouse International, 1979.
10. Radebaugh, Lee H. "Environmental Factors Influencing the Development of Accounting Objectives, Standards, and Practices in Peru." *International Journal of Accounting,* Fall 1975.
11. Tyra, Anita I. "Financial Disclosure Patterns in Four European Countries." *International Journal of Accounting,* Spring 1970.

Chapter 2

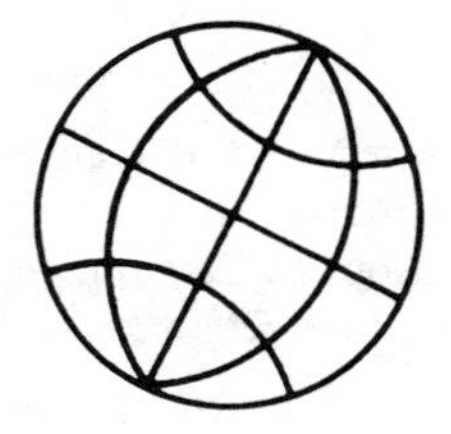

Accounting Policy Formulation[1]

Throughout most of the world, accounting regulations have long been recognized as a means of enhancing the reliability of accounting reports. By reducing alternative accounting practices, accounting regulations help to eliminate abuses and injustices in the accounting field. Such regulations also help ensure that accounting reports are of real value to their users, including investors, creditors, governments, labor, and management.

How regulations develop varies from country to country. The accounting profession has taken the lead in developing accounting regulations in some countries, while in others, regulations are imposed upon the accounting profession by legislative bodies. In still other countries, both the accounting profession and governmental agencies work together to set accounting regulations. The determining factors as to who actually establishes accounting regulations appear to be (1) the status and the size of the accounting profession in the country, and (2) the degree to which the government seeks to control economic activity. For example, the relatively small size of the accounting profession in the

[1]Much of the material in this chapter draws on information contained in the international publications (the country guides) of the large international accounting firms.

nations of Asia, Africa, continental Europe, and Latin America, combined with significant degrees of government control over their economic sectors, had led in these places to the legislation of accounting standards and procedures. In Anglo-American countries, on the other hand, accounting standards and procedures have been developed largely by the accounting profession itself, with somewhat less input by governments.

This chapter reviews accounting policy formulation and regulation in several countries, focusing on both similarities and differences. It also describes efforts by several organizations to lessen or eliminate national differences in accounting policies, procedures, and practices. These efforts come under the rubric of "harmonization."

FINANCIAL REGULATION IN THE UNITED STATES

In the United States, accounting is regulated both by the accounting profession and by legislation. The American Institute of Certified Public Accountants (AICPA) and the Financial Accounting Standards Board (FASB) have coordinated private sector efforts to regulate the practice of accounting in the country. Statements are issued establishing accounting and auditing standards to which members of the AICPA should adhere in their accounting practices.

The U.S. Uniform Commercial Code, on the other hand, does not contain any requirements specifying how corporations must maintain their accounting books. Instead, state laws determine minimal record-keeping requirements. In addition, the government's Securities and Exchange Commission (SEC) has issued Regulation S-X and Accounting Series Releases specifying the form and content for the financial statements of publicly-held corporations, including income statements, balance sheets, and statements of changes in financial position. Finally, tax laws certainly have had major effects on the accounting practices of the U.S.

Legislation for Financial Reporting

The SEC, mentioned above, perhaps has the most significant legislative authority over the establishment of accounting standards and procedures in the United States. Under Section 19 (a) of the Securities Act of

1933, the SEC can standardize accounting terminology, accounting measurement, and accounting reporting. However, the SEC historically has been reluctant to exercise its power fully, since it believes that the accounting profession should be allowed to police itself. The SEC requires that financial statements of publicly held corporations be prepared in accordance with the "generally accepted accounting principles" adopted by the accounting profession. In addition, the SEC requires detailed supplementary schedules to support financial statements. Finally, annual financial statements filed with the SEC are to be accompanied by an auditors' report.

All publicly-held corporations are required to have their annual financial statements audited by a professional accounting firm. The AICPA, in cooperation with the different state boards of accountancy, specifies the requirements that individuals should fulfill in order to be considered professional accountants (auditors). The laws of the different states generally require that corporations hold annual stockholders meetings during which the stockholders approve both the financial statements and the auditors' report.

The Accounting Profession's Role

Accounting flexibility has been the official attitude of the accounting profession in the United States, as evidenced by the actions of the American Institute of Certified Public Accountants and the Financial Accounting Standards Board. As early as 1932, a special committee of the AICPA took the following position in a report to the New York Stock Exchange on the variety of and lack of consistency in the accounting practices of the time:

> In considering ways of improving the existing situation two alternatives suggest themselves. The first is the selection by competent authority out of the body of acceptable methods in vogue today of detailed sets of rules which would become binding on all corporations of a given class. . . . The arguments against any attempt to apply this alternative to industrial corporations generally are, however, overwhelming.
>
> The more practicable alternative would be to leave every corporation free to choose its own methods of accounting within the very broad limits to which reference has been made, but require disclosure of the methods employed and consistency in their application from year to year.[2]

[2]American Institute of Accountants, *Audits of Corporate Accounts* (New York: AIA, 1934), p. 7.

Accounting flexibility has always had its critics. For example, while serving as Chairman of the SEC, Carman Blough made this observation in 1937:

> An examination of hundreds of statements filed with our Commission almost leads one to the conclusion that aside from simple rules of double entry bookkeeping, there are very few principles of accounting upon which the accountants in this country are in agreement.[3]

Along with certain abuses which existed during the 1920s and 1930s, the dismay at the lack of uniformity may help to explain why the SEC played a major role in accounting regulation through the issuance of its Accounting Series Releases during the 1930s and 1940s. Since the late 1940s, however, the SEC has allowed the accounting profession to undertake the formation of its own accounting standards and procedures.

But the SEC's reliance on the accounting profession to establish accounting standards and procedures may not continue because of new abuses and injustices found in the accounting field. The accounting profession recently has been attacked by some U.S. Congressmen for its failure to cure abuses in the field. Thus, the SEC is presently under pressure to exercise its power and to play a more active role in developing accounting regulations.

FINANCIAL REGULATION IN THE UNITED KINGDOM

Accounting regulation in the United Kingdom can be found in both professional pronouncements ("Statements of Standard Accounting Practice"), and legislation ("Companies Acts"). The former statements are prepared by the Institute of Chartered Accountants in England and Wales, along with other major accounting bodies in the country, and serve to supplement the requirements of the Companies Acts as to the form and content of financial statements. The provision of these statements are mandatory for practicing accountants, and any departure from them must be disclosed in the auditors' report. In addition, the Institute issues accounting standards for its members, "Recommenda-

[3]Carman G. Blough, "Need for Accounting Principles," *The Accounting Review* (March 1937), p. 31.

tions on Accounting Principles," to guide them in practice, and these recommendations are normally followed.

Unlike most countries in the European Community, tax laws have little effect on accounting standards and procedures in the United Kingdom. In general, according to these laws, "generally accepted accounting standards" can be used as a basis for determining the taxable income of a corporation.

Legislation for Financial Reporting

At the present time, corporations are regulated by the Companies Acts of 1948 and 1967. These Acts require all corporations to keep "proper books of account," which should contain the information necessary to give a "true and fair view" of the company's financial affairs. In addition, each corporation is required to prepare a profit and loss account (income statement) and a balance sheet at the end of each accounting period. These financial statements, along with the directors' report and the auditors' report, must be prepared within nine months prior to the date of the annual general meeting of the stockholders. This general meeting must be held in each calendar year, with not more than fifteen months between meetings. A company which has one subsidiary or more is usually required to prepare consolidated statements.

Companies Acts mandate the appointment of a quality auditor for each corporation. Auditors are usually appointed by the stockholders at the annual general meeting. Individuals can be considered for appointment as auditors if they are members of one of the accounting bodies recognized for this purpose by the Department of Trade. In addition, a person may be authorized by the Department of Trade to be an auditor if it is deemed that he obtained similar credentials outside the United Kingdom (a CPA from the United States, for example, would qualify under this provision). The auditors' report should state whether financial statements were prepared in conformity with the Companies Acts of 1948 and 1967, and whether they give a "true and fair view" of the company's financial position and the results of its operations.

The Accounting Profession's Role

The accounting bodies whose members are qualified by the Department of Trade as auditors include: (1) the Institute of Chartered Accountants in England and Wales; (2) the Institute of Chartered Accountants of

Scotland; (3) the Institute of Chartered Accountants in Ireland; and (4) the Association of Certified Accountants. These four bodies, in addition to the Institute of Cost and Management Accountants and the Chartered Institute of Public Finance and Accountancy, have formed joint committees to promote proper accounting standards (the Accounting Standards Committee), to advance auditing practices (the Auditing Practices Committee), and to present the views of the accounting profession (the Consultative Committee of Accountancy Bodies).

The Institute of Chartered Accountants in England and Wales issues "Recommendations on Accounting Principles" to guide its members. While departure from these recommendations does not necessarily require disclosure, these recommendations usually have been applied in practice. For the most part, accounting standards and procedures have been developed gradually in the United Kingdom due to the cooperative efforts of both the government and the accounting profession. The latter is actively involved in preparing governmental legislation that concerns accounting matters.

FINANCIAL REGULATION IN BRAZIL

Accounting practices in Brazil are basically those described by the Brazilian Commercial Code, the Corporation Law of December 15, 1976, regulations of the Central Bank, and the tax laws. As with other developing nations, governmental regulation in Brazil plays a significant role in accounting matters because of the comparatively small size of the accounting profession. The Brazilian Institute of Independent Auditors, in fact, plays a very minor role in establishing national accounting standards and procedures.

Legislation for Financial Reporting

A corporation, called a *sociedade anônima* (or an "anonymous society"), is governed by the Corporation Law No. 6404 of December 15, 1976. This law, applicable to all corporations and groups of companies, requires the preparation of the income statement, the retained earnings statement, the statement of changes in financial position, and the balance sheet. In addition, it requires the preparation of consolidated statements for groups of companies, and the use of the equity method for nonconsolidated subsidiaries.

Aritcle 4 of the 1976 Corporation Law defines a publicly owned corporation (an open corporation) as ". . . one which, subject to prior registration with the Securities Commission, has its issued securities admitted for dealing on the stock market or over-the-counter market." According to this law, the annual stockholders' meeting of this open corporation should be held within four months from the end of the accounting period. During the meeting, stockholders approve the annual correction of capital (the monetary correction system will be discussed in Chapter 4). The annual financial statements of publicly owned corporations must comply with the rules laid down by the *Comissao de Vabres Mobiliarios* (the Securities Commission), and must be audited by independent auditors registered with this Commission. At least a month before the annual meeting, management is required by law to have made available to the stockholders its report on the activities of the company, the annual financial statements, and the report of the independent auditors.

The 1976 Corporation Law also delineates certain aspects of a corporation's organizational structure. For example, an open corporation should have a minimum of three members who form an "administrative council" to define policy, to lay down guidelines for the activities of the company, and to appoint independent auditors. In addition, an open corporation is required to have a "board of directors," composed of two or more members, for executing policies of the administrative council.

The Commercial Code requires, from all corporations and individuals conducting business transactions in the country, the maintenance of a proper set of accounting books, each of which would differ depending upon the nature of the business activities represented by those books. The principal accounting book is the journal (*Diario*) in which all business transactions are recorded. In addition, other accounting books, considered subsidiary, are offered as supplements to the information contained in the journal.

The Accounting Profession's Role

As mentioned earlier, the Brazilian Institute of Independent Auditors plays only a small role in establishing accounting standards and procedures in the country. The accounting profession in Brazil is too small and lacks the power and status to influence accounting matters to any significant degree. In addition, Brazil's desire for rapid economic growth and the need to control both the direction of that growth and its side-effects (for example, inflation) have resulted in highly authoritarian styles of governance. Thus, the Brazilian government plays the major role in establishing accounting standards and procedures.

FINANCIAL REGULATION IN FRANCE

Financial accounting in France is greatly influenced by legislation due mainly to the determination of the French government to obtain data for economic planning and, more recently, for social accounting purposes. To underscore these concerns of the French government, French tax law permits the deductibility of expenses only if they are included in the financial statements of enterprises. In addition, the 1947 *Plan Comptable General* (Uniform Chart of Accounts), containing a detailed chart of accounts and a series of model financial and statistical reports needed for micro and macro accounting purposes, has been adopted by virtually all enterprises in the country.

Legislation for Financial Reporting

The 1947 *Plan Comptable Général* was the first comprehensive effort to regulate accounting in France, an effort made by the National Council of Accountancy (NCA). This Plan specifies accounting definitions, standards, procedures, and the forms of financial statements. The Plan continues to be revised to respond to the changing needs of society.

A French corporation, known either as a *Société Anonyme* (S.A.) or as a *Société à Responsabilité Limitée (S.A.R.L.)*, is governed by provisions of the Law on Commercial Companies of July 24, 1966, as modified on March 23, 1967. Under the 1966 law, a report by management on the activities of the company, a trading account, a profit and loss account, and a balance sheet should be prepared at the end of each accounting period. The publication of consolidated financial statements is not required of corporations. The 1967 law added that financial statements be submitted to the auditors of the corporation forty-five days before the annual general meeting. The 1966 law also regulates the appointment and the responsibilities of auditors.

Under the 1966 law, an S.A. may be managed by a board of directors (*conseil d'administration*) and a president (*president-directeur-general*). The board of directors elect the president who is responsible for the operational management of the company. Although individuals representing employees may attend the meetings of the board of directors, they do not have voting privileges.

The specific accounting regulations related to an S.A. are as follows:

1. The board of directors should prepare its report on the activities of the company, a trading account, a profit and loss account, and a balance sheet at the end of each accounting period.

2. Financial statements should be prepared in accordance with French accounting standards and disclosure requirements. These accounting standards have emerged from the pronouncements of the professional accounting bodies, the 1966 law, and the *Plan Comptable General.*

3. Statutory auditors are appointed by stockholders in their annual meetings for a term of six years. These auditors not only express their opinion on the *fairness* of financial statements, but also comment on the health of the company as a whole. In their report to the stockholders, statutory auditors refer to the fact that the audit work was carried out in accordance with 1966 law and with other tests based on generally accepted auditing standards which are deemed necessary. In addition, if during the course of their examination these auditors discover that the company violated the law, they are required to report that violation to the Prosecutor.

4. The Commercial Code requires commercial entities to maintain a general journal (*livre journal*) in which business transactions are recorded, a detailed list (*livre d'inventaire*) of the assets and liabilities, and copies of all correspondence.

5. The Labor Code requires commercial entities to maintain a payroll journal (*livre de paye*) in which is recorded the information shown on each individual pay slip.

6. The *livre journal*, the *livre d'inventaire*, and the *livre de paye* should be prenumbered, stamped by a court or similar authority, and be maintained without blanks or erasures.

The Accounting Profession's Role

The accounting profession in France has been actively involved in the preparation of legislation related to accounting matters, which explains the historical readiness of the accounting profession to adopt accounting legislation. The accounting standards and procedures adopted in France are those prescribed by the French *Plan*, the tax Decree of October 28, 1965, the laws of July 24, 1966 and March 23, 1967 mentioned above, and the Finance Acts of 1977 and 1978. Professional institutes, however, have continued to issue numerous recommendations on proper accounting guidelines in order to implement and to revise the *Plan Comptable Général* and to encourage revision of the tax laws. The National Association of Certified Accountants and the National Council of Accountancy, for example, are two such groups issuing opinions and guidelines.

A conservative doctrine is dominant within the accounting profession in France, partly due to the fact that officers of a corporation can be held legally liable for the failure of the organization to generate profits. This legal liability also partially explains the popularity of numerous accounting reserves, a subject described in greater detail in Chapter 3.

FINANCIAL REGULATION IN GERMANY

Accounting in Germany, as in France, is heavily influenced by legislation. In fact, most of accounting standards and procedures applied in Germany are prescribed by law. Sources of accounting regulation can be found in the Commercial Code (*Handelsgesetz*), the Corporation Act (*Aktiengesetz*), the Cooperatives Act (*Genossenschaftsgesetz*), and other laws related to specific types of business.

Legislation for Financial Reporting

The Commercial Code requires business entities: (1) to maintain books of accounts in accordance with the "principles of proper bookkeeping (*Grundsaetze ordnungsmaessiger Buchfuehrung*)"; (2) to prepare annual financial statements; and (3) to retain the company's books and correspondence for a specific period of time. Paragraph 38 of this Code states:

> Every merchant is obliged to keep books and to show therein his business transactions and his financial situation in conformity with the principles of proper accounting.

Sections 149 and 151 to 159 of the Corporation Act of 1965 set forth the accounting standards and procedures that should be utilized in the preparation of financial statements.

Other legislation specifies such matters as the following: (1) disclosure standards for companies; (2) when and what type of financial statements should be published; and (3) other details related to classification and reporting requirements. The Publicity Law, for example, requires businesses with a balance sheet total exceeding DM125 million and an annual sales of more than DM250 million, on three consecutive year-end dates, to publish their financial statements. These statements include the profit and loss statement and the balance sheet, accompanied with a report from management on the activities of the company.[4] A corporation (an *Aktiengesellschaft*, or *A.G.*) is further required under Sections 331 and 332 of the Corporation Act to publish consolidated statements if the management of the A.G. has control over the operations of other companies and owns more than 50% of their common stock. These consolidated statements are generally limited to domestic subsidiaries, however.

The annual financial statements and management report of an A.G. are prepared and submitted to the company's statutory independent public accountant (*Wirtschaftsprüfer*) for examination within three months after the end of the accounting period. An A.G. may have one or more auditors who are elected by stockholders at their annual meeting. The report of the auditors should disclose whether financial statements are prepared in accordance with the provisions of the law, and whether the management's report helps to give a true picture of the company's affairs. Upon the completion of this examination, management is required to submit to a supervisory board the annual financial statements, its report, and the auditors' report for its approval. For an A.G. with less than 2000 employees, one third of the membership of this board should represent the employees, while the other two thirds are elected by the stockholders; with employees of 2000 or more, labor is equally represented on this board alongside those elected by the stockholders.

The Accounting Profession's Role

Over the years the accounting profession in Germany has developed "principles of proper bookkeeping." These standards, however, are not equivalent to the "generally accepted accounting principles" in the United States. In Germany, the "generally accepted accounting principles" are standards prescribed by law. Thus, German accounting practitioners are concerned with complying with the laws that prescribe accounting standards and procedures more than they are concerned with developing those standards and procedures. As a result of

[4]An average annual number of employees of over 5,000 individuals may substitute for one of the above two conditions.

a general bias towards protecting creditors, the accounting standards in Germany lead to the preparation of financial statements which do not necessarily serve the needs of investors, stockholders, or other interested parties. Recent reforms of company laws in Germany, however, have brought accounting standards much closer to those the German business community would like to see.

Extreme conservatism in the valuation of assets and in determining income is permitted in Germany. For example, the establishment of secret or hidden reserves is both permitted and encouraged by law in order to protect creditors. In addition, accounting practitioners tend to put more emphasis on the form than on the substance of financial statements precisely because accounting is so highly legislated.

FINANCIAL REGULATION IN JAPAN

Japanese financial accounting regulations have been patterned largely on U.S. and German accounting regulations. In addition, the tax laws in Japan have greatly influenced the accounting practices there, for example, in the calculation of depreciation charges, in the allowance for doubtful accounts, and in the estimated liability for warranty expense.

"Business accounting principles" were officially introduced in Japan in 1949 by the Economic Stabilization Board. Under these regulations, Japanese corporations must maintain proper books of accounts and prepare the profit and loss statement, the balance sheet, and many other supplementary schedules. In addition, since April 1, 1977, all listed corporations in the country have been required to prepare consolidated financial statements. The use of the equity method of accounting for carrying the investment account on the books of the parent company, however, is optional, and the consolidation requirement applies only to affiliates owned 51% or more by the parent company. Because most Japanese firms own less than 51% of these subsidiaries' stock, the subsidiaries more often are carried as investments rather than being consolidated.

Legislation for Financial Reporting

Article 32 of the Commercial Code, as amended by Ministry of Finance Regulation No. 54 of September 28, 1974, attempts to ensure that "fair and just accounting conventions shall be taken into consideration in interpretation of provisions concerning the preparation of accounting books." This Code requires that all business entities maintain a double-entry bookkeeping system, with a general ledger and subledgers. All listed companies must also file their annual audited financial statements with the Ministry of Finance.

Under the Commercial Code, a public company (*Kabushika Kaisha* or *Yugen Kaisha*) is required to have a statutory auditor elected by stockholders in the general meeting. The auditor, who is not required to be a professional accountant, acts as a watchdog and is responsible for examining the financial statements of the company and reporting any violations of the law and/or of the articles of incorporation of the company. In addition, under the 1976 Law Concerning Special Exceptions to the Commercial Code Relating to Audit, companies with a capital of 1 billion yen or more, companies listed on the Japanese stock exchanges, or companies making specific public distribution of their shares are each required to have independent public accountants (professionals appointed by the board of directors).

The profit and loss statement, the balance sheet, the statutory auditor's report, the directors' report, and the report of the independent auditor (if any) are required to be sent to stockholders at least two weeks before the periodic general meeting (which is either semiannual or annual) for their approval.

The Accounting Profession's Role

The Ministry of Finance exercises significant control over the accounting profession in Japan. It sets the accounting standards to be carried out by the profession through the publication of "Business Accounting Principles and Auditing Standards." Furthermore, the Ministry can even establish a fee structure which is binding on all independent auditors.

The Certified Public Accountants Law of 1948 established the foundation for the Japanese Institute of Certified Public Accountants. This Institute has been involved mainly in setting the professional qualifications for CPAs. In addition, the Institute issues statements, called "Notes," on auditing procedures and rules of conduct for the profession.

By U.S. standards, the accounting profession in Japan is often overconservative. This can be seen, for example, in the highly accelerated depreciation practiced by the Japanese in their "inventory price fluctuation reserves," and in their allowances for doubtful accounts. These charges are normally allowed for tax purposes.

FINANCIAL REGULATION IN THE NETHERLANDS

Accounting practices in the Netherlands are not as heavily influenced by legislation as they are in other continental European countries or in Japan. Rather than a system of legislation specifying accounting standards and procedures to be utilized by businesses, the Commercial Code (*Wetboeck van Koophandel*) merely requires that proper books of accounts be maintained by all enterprises and that accounting be based on "sound business practice." The Financial Statements Act of 1970 (*Wet op de Jaarrekening van Ondernemingen*) establishes the requirements for the preparation of financial statements at the end of each accounting period, under which a parent company may prepare consolidated financial statements. The lack of specific legislation regulating accounting standards and procedures in the Netherlands gives the Dutch accounting profession great flexibility in developing sound accounting standards and procedures.

Legislation for Financial Reporting

There are two types of legal forms for a corporation in the Netherlands, namely, the public limited liability company (*Naamloze Vennootschap*, abbreviated, *N.V.*) and the private limited liability company (*Besloten Vennootschap*, abbreviated *B.V.*). These two forms for a corporation are similar to those that exist in other European countries such as France and Germany. Under the Commercial Code, each N.V. and B.V. is required to prepare a profit and loss statement and a balance sheet at the end of its accounting period. In addition, Article 2 of the Financial Statements Act of 1970 requires that

> the financial statements provide such information that a sound judgment can be formed on the financial position and the results of operations and, to the extent to which financial statements permit, on its solvency and liquidation.

And Article 5 of this Act prescribes that

> the bases underlying the valuation of the assets and liabilities and the determination of the results of operations comply with standards that are regarded as being acceptable in economic and social life.

These stipulations leave the accounting profession a great measure of latitude in the preparation of financial statements. The bases of valuation can be any of the various approaches to valuation available in practice, as long as they are "acceptable in economic and social life" and as long as they assist the readers of financial statements in making "a sound judgment" on the enterprise.

Under the Commercial Code and the Financial Statements Act of 1970, all N.V.'s (excluding subsidiaries of Dutch companies included in the report of another corporation and meeting specific conditions) and certain B.V.'s (for example, those with capital stock of more than f500,000, or with total assets of at least f8,000,000 and at least 100 employees) are required to have an annual audit by professional accountants. These professional auditors must be members of the Netherlands Institute of Registered Accountants (NIVRA) or persons permitted by the Minister of Economic Affairs to practice as auditors. The 1970 Act requires auditors to disclose in their reports any noncompliance with the Act.

The management of each company is required to prepare the profit and loss statement and the balance sheet within five months after the end of the accounting period. For major companies, these statements, and the auditor's report if applicable, must be submitted to the supervisory board of directors (*Raad van Commissarissen*) for their acceptance, who in turn submit the statements to the stockholders' annual meeting for final approval. These statements are also submitted to the Works Council (for employers with at least 100 employees) for the purposes of discussion and information only.

The Accounting Profession's Role

The passage of the Registered Accountants Act, which became effective in 1963, established NIVRA, which makes it a semi-governmental professional accounting body. NIVRA has issued a code of ethics and auditing standards for the profession similar to those issued in the United Kingdom and the United States.

NIVRA has been actively involved in those legislative processes related to accounting. For example, it welcomed the passage of the 1970 Act which specified a series of examinations for an individual who wishes to become a registered accountant and join NIVRA.

Accounting in the Netherlands is closely tied to business economics, a factor which has had a major effect on the development of accounting standards in the country, and which is evident in the use of replacement value by major corporations such as Philips N.V. Since it is believed that the preparation of financial statements based on the replacement value concept helps readers to make "a sound judgment" on the enterprise, the use of the concept is becoming prevalent in the Netherlands. NIVRA fully supports the use of this concept for financial reporting purposes, which also encourages its popularity.

FINANCIAL REGULATION IN SWITZERLAND

Accounting in Switzerland is influenced by the Code of Obligations (*Obligationenrecht*) and the tax laws. For example, according to the tax laws, expenses cannot be deducted for tax purposes unless they have been recorded in the accounting books, a situation consistent with the practices of other Continental European countries. In addition, uniform accounting systems have been developed for many industries in Switzerland, and have proven to be flexible enough to accommodate the different needs of enterprises. Though voluntary, their use is fairly widespread, resulting in a formal standardization of Swiss accounting standards and procedures.

Legislation for Financial Reporting

The influence of legislation on accounting is minimal. The only legislation in Switzerland which deals with accounting and financial reporting is the Code of Obligations. The requirements of this Code are so general as to invite very broad interpretations. Under this Code, companies must keep accounting books, for example, in accordance with the "character and extent" of the business, showing the financial position and results of operations of the business (Article 957). Financial statements should be prepared "completely, clearly and plainly in accordance with recognized commercial principles, so that interested parties may inform themselves as accurately as possible of the economic position of the business" (Article 959).

The Code of Obligations regulates publicly held corporations (*Aktiengesellschaft*, abbreviated *A.G.*) and privately held companies (*Gesellschaft mit beschränkter Haftung*, abbreviated *GmbH*). Each corporation is required to prepare a profit and loss statement and a balance sheet at the end of each accounting period. Only minimum disclosure is required in these statements and extreme conservatism is encouraged by the Code (for example, formation and organization costs are expensed and charged against the revenues of the period). In addition, requirements for the preparation of consolidated financial statements and statements of changes in financial position do not exist.

A.G.'s are required to have one or more statutory auditors (*Kontrollstelle*) who are elected by the stockholders at the annual general meeting. Although no professional qualifications are required for this position, statutory auditors must be able to examine financial statements to be sure that they are prepared in accordance with the valuation standards set forth in the Code and the Company's by-laws. Furthermore, the responsibility of these auditors extends to the community regarding the performance of management during the accounting period. If an A.G. has capital of SFrs. 5 million or more, bonds outstanding, or has invited the public to entrust money to it, its financial statements must also be examined by an independent professional accountant appointed by the board of directors (Article 723). The report of this independent auditor should be submitted to the board of directors and to the statutory auditors.

An annual stockholders' general meeting must be held within six months after the end of the accounting period. At the general meeting, management is required to submit for the stockholders' approval the financial statements, along with the report of the statutory auditors.

The Accounting Profession's Role

Although the Code of Obligations does not require auditors to have any special expertise, auditing is normally done by members of the Society of Swiss Certified Accountants (*Verband Schweizerischer Bücherexpaten*, abbreviated *VSB*), independent professional accountants who are mostly organized into corporations (fiduciary companies).

The VSB is a division of the Swiss Chamber of Fiduciary Auditors. Regarding accounting matters, the Chamber publishes recommendations which are not binding on auditors. It has also issued a code of ethics and a set of auditing standards that its members are expected to follow.

As indicated above, Switzerland does enjoy flexibility in accounting standards and procedures. At the same time, the conservatism that prevails in Switzerland tends toward only the minimal disclosure sufficient to protect outside interests and to ensure that no overstatement of assets occurs. The prevailing continental European approach involving codified minimum accounting requirements also applies in Switzerland. Corporations which voluntarily exceed these requirements frequently follow an approach similar to that found in other German-speaking countries, for example, the utilization of secret reserves to protect creditors.

THE HARMONIZATION OF ACCOUNTING

Many scholars have suggested that in order to create an international comparability of accounting reports, a worldwide harmonization of accounting standards and procedures should be encouraged. To answer this need, three models of accounting have been identified and discussed in the literature: (1) the *Absolute Uniformity Model,* which suggests that there be one set of accounting methods and reports regardless of differences in circumstances or user needs; (2) the *Circumstantial Uniformity Model,* which suggests that different accounting methods and reports be used for varying economic facts under different conditions; and (3) the *Purposive Uniformity Model,* which considers the uses of accounting information as determinants of the appropriate accounting methods, standards, and reports (See Exhibit 2.1).

While the first model has the appeal of administrative ease, it has not been enthusiastically accepted by free-enterprise societies, probably because it appears too radical and too inflexible. The second model was proposed in 1965 by a special committee of the American Institute of Certified Public Accountants (AICPA) in order to reduce alternative practices in accounting. In making its report to AICPA, the special committee furnished an example:

> The field of medicine provides an analogy. The doctor may encounter the same disease in patients, but a variation in treatment is applied where the attending circumstances are different. So also in accounting the circumstances surrounding the application of a given principle may be substantially different. That is what justifies and even necessitates variations.[5]

In 1978 the chairman of the U.S. Financial Accounting Standards Board (FASB), Donald J. Kirk, stated that the FASB was striving to account for similar situations in a similar way and not to make dissimilar sit-

[5]American Institute of Certified Public Accountants, *Report of Special Committee on Opinions of the Accounting Principles Board* (New York: AICPA, Spring 1965), p. 17.

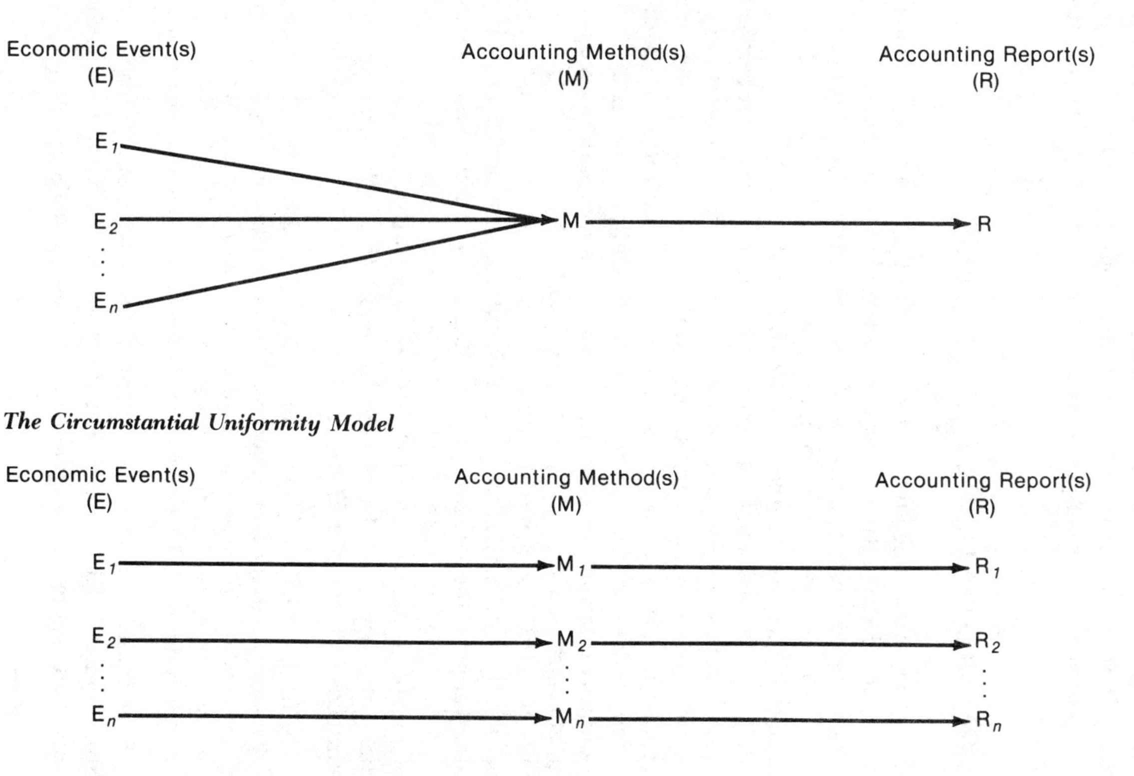

EXHIBIT 2.1 *Accounting Uniformity Models*

The Purposive Uniformity Model

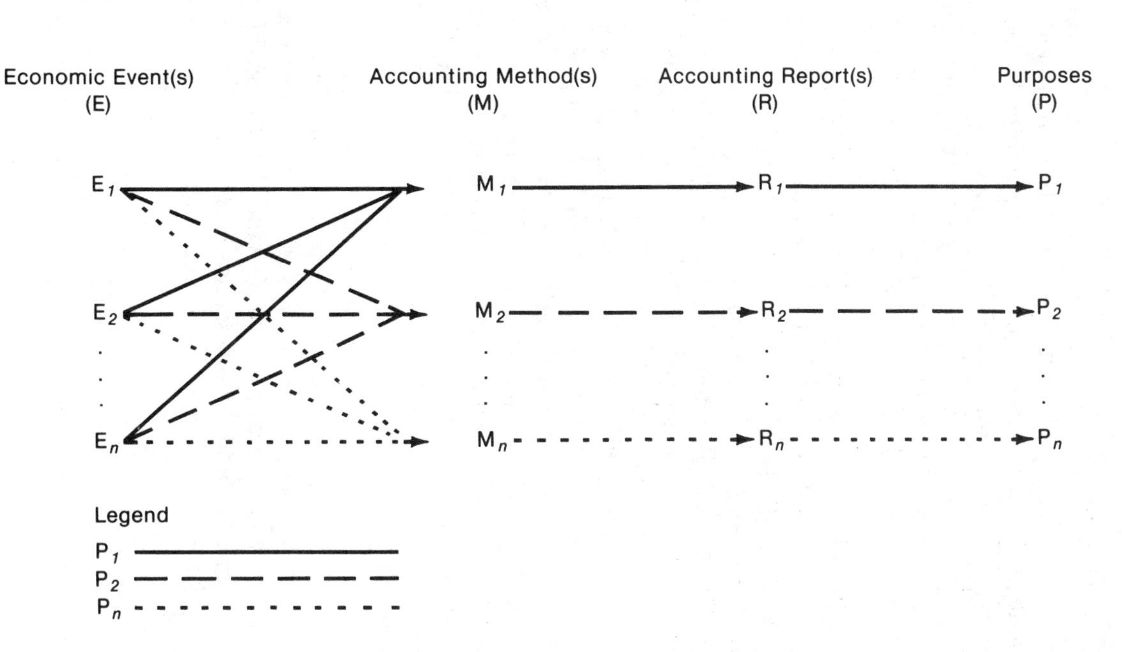

EXHIBIT 2.1 *Accounting Uniformity Models (continued)*

uations look alike.[6] Thus, it seems that the accounting profession in the U.S. is moving toward the adoption of the Circumstantial Uniformity Model.

The concept of the Purposive Uniformity Model is utilitarian: the uses of the accounting information dictate the appropriate accounting methods, standards, and reports. Examples of such methods and standards being matched to the use include different accounting methods used in pricing inventory (such as first-in-first-out, or last-in-first-out) for different cost flows, and different accounting standards (such as historical-cost or replacement-cost) applied for different user needs (that is, preparing financial statements for creditors, investors, managers, and so on).

The main difference between the Circumstantial and the Purposive Uniformity Models is that the former is flexible for different circumstances, whereas the latter is flexible for both different circumstances and different purposes. Under the Purposive Uniformity Model, different purposes (or needs) demand the use of certain accounting standards, and different circumstances (sets of facts) demand the use of certain accounting procedures, each of which accurately reflects the application of an accounting standard under a specified set of facts. The Circumstantial Uniformity Model, on the other hand, suggests that once different sets of circumstances have been identified—as islands of truth—then appropriate accounting methods and standards would follow *ipso facto* from those circumstances apart from the purposes of the users of accounting information. The Purposive Uniformity Model is descriptive of regulatory practice in the U.S., and underlies accounting in most socialist countries as well.

It is clear that when talking about the harmonization of accounting standards, a person needs to specify the model he is following in order to communicate better with others. Here we wish to emphasize that differences in environmental forces demand the use of different accounting systems. Exhibit 2.2 schematically represents how accounting postulates, concepts, and standards fit into a context of cultural, social, political, legal, and economic conditions.

Accounting postulates derived from the free-enterprise environment are necessarily different from those derived from other environments, such as a centrally controlled economy. Using the deductive approach,

---

[6]Deloitte Haskins & Sells, "The Chairman Speaks," *The Week in Review* (March 17, 1978), p. 1.

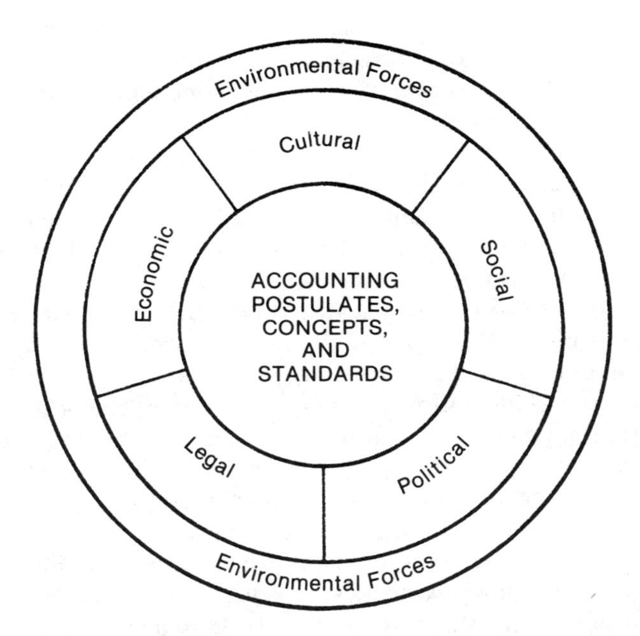

EXHIBIT 2.2 *The Environmental Forces Influencing Accounting Postulates and Standards*

accounting standards developed from a set of free-enterprise postulates should differ from those derived from other sets of postulates. In some countries of the world, accounting is even thought of as an instrument of national economic policy.

In Sweden, for example, it is considered a good accounting practice to provide for investment fund reserves in profitable years (up to 40% of profit before tax), and then to use these funds in periods when the economy is under stress. Thus, corporations can avoid up to 40% of their annual tax bill through the establishment of these funds. To benefit from these anticyclical investment funds, companies have to deposit 46% of the allocated funds in noninterest-bearing accounts in the central bank (*Sveriges Riksbank*), that is, about what is actually saved in tax. These funds cannot be used by corporations without the approval of the Labour Market Board. Based on the needs of the economy, this Board then decides when and for what purposes these funds can be used. However, after five years of its deposit in the central bank, a company can withdraw 30% of the amount on deposit without the prior approval of the board. Upon the release of the funds, corporations can take additional tax deductions equal to 10% of the funds released. Despite this provision, a corporation cannot claim depreciation expense on the asset purchased out of these funds, which would result in an increase in its future taxes.

In socialist countries, the main objective of accounting is to facilitate national planning and control. This explains the tendency in these countries toward accounting uniformity, since it is difficult, if not impossible, for a central government to find out which sector of the economy is lagging in efficiency or productivity without comparable accounting information. The Egyptian Uniform Accounting Law of 1966 is an example of the uniformity regulations typical in these countries. Based on this uniform system of accounts, financial and social accounting are coordinated in order to facilitate the determination of the Gross National Product and other statistical data used to analyze the economy and to control its direction. Exhibit 2.3 A–E shows the financial statements of an Egyptian company.

The uniform system of accounts, however, is not peculiar to socialist countries in the third world (less developed nations). In France, for example, accounting standards and methods used by enterprises are also based on a uniform system of accounts called, as you will remember, the "*Plan Comptable Général*" which was enacted in 1946 (see pp. 25–27). The *Plan*, used by virtually all enterprises in the country, contains a detailed chart of accounts and a series of model financial and statistical reports needed for micro- and macro-accounting purposes.

Efforts to Establish International Accounting Standards

Progress has been slow toward the development and implementation of international accounting standards and reports. In order to establish a forum for an exchange of ideas, the First International Congress of Accountants was held in the United States in 1904. Subsequent conferences have been held periodically in different parts of the world, but without any significant accomplishments. Two noteworthy developments, however, did occur at the Tenth International Congress of Accountants held in Sydney, Australia in 1972. The first was the formation of the International Accounting Standards Committee (IASC), and the second, the establishment of the International Coordination Committee for the Accounting Profession (ICCAP). In June 1973, representatives of professional accounting bodies from Australia, Canada, France, Japan, Mexico, the Netherlands, the United Kingdom, Ireland, the United States, and West Germany met in London to establish the IASC. The membership of this Committee has since increased through the association of professional accounting bodies from other countries. As of January 1983, the total number of accounting organizations participating in the IASC was 88 and represented 62 different countries.

The basic objective of the IASC is to formulate *international accounting standards* to be observed in the preparation of financial statements. From its establishment in 1973 until the present, the IASC has issued nineteen definite International Accounting Standards and twenty-five Exposure Drafts (see Exhibit 2.4.) Members of the Committee have committed themselves to introducing these standards in their respective countries. However, since the IASC has no powers of enforcement, adherence to these standards has been far from complete. Several factors are involved—some accounting bodies simply do not *have* the power to enforce their standards in their countries; still others want to wait until they are sure that these standards are internationally accepted. Thus, the possibility for a set of international accounting standards is troubled by problems, and the IASC has only been moderately successful in its efforts at harmonization.

The ICCAP and IFAC

The ICCAP was established with the objective of developing and enhancing a coordinated worldwide accountancy profession with *harmonized auditing standards.* The ICCAP was composed of representatives from Australia, Canada, France, India, Japan, Mexico, the Netherlands, the Philippines, the United Kingdom, Ireland, the United States, and West Germany. In February 1976, the ICCAP sent an interim report to ninety-nine professional accounting bodies, recommending its own replacement by a more permanent worldwide organization to be based in New York and called the International Federation of Accountants (IFAC). This proposal was considered and adopted by the delegates at the Eleventh International Congress of Accountants held in Munich on October 10, 1977. The main objective of the IFAC is to work toward establishing international standards of auditing, ethics, education, and training, leaving the formation of inter-

(Text is continued on page 53.)

EXHIBIT 2.3A *Alnaser Company BALANCE SHEET (As of June 30, 1971)*

1969–1970 Egyptian Pounds	Uniform Account No.		Egyptian Pounds	Egyptian Pounds
19,230,195	211–212	Capital		19,780,195
		Appropriations & Profits		
18,971	226	Appropriations for increase in assets' prices . .	33,188	
161,888	227	Other appropriations	209,437	
	228	Profits for the period	81,097	323,722
180,859				
		Allowances		
4,983,990	231	Allowance for depreciation	5,529,563	
	232	Allowance for disputed taxes . . .	20,000	
20,062	233	Allowance for doubtful accounts	20,062	
728,665	234	Other allowances	2,006,276	7,575,901
5,732,717				

1969–1970 Egyptian Pounds	Uniform Account No.		Egyptian Pounds	Egyptian Pounds
		Fixed Assets		
132,743	111	Land	132,743	
2,421,962	112	Bldg., construction & roads. . .	2,889,524	
5,011,954	113	Equipment	5,098,957	
519,906	114	Cars	544,080	
79,222	115	Tools	90,940	
57,166	116	Furniture.	64,093	
2,108,937	118	Deferred revenue expenditures . .	2,446,678	11,267,015
10,331,890				

Previous year	Account	Item		Current year
		Long-term Liabilities		
1,500,000	241	Local long-term loans	4,000,000	
6,090,038	242	Foreign long-term loans	4,968,025	8,968,025
7,590,038				
1,719,066	251	Bank overdraft . .	2,693,826	
5,991,798	261–263	Creditors	5,941,086	
2,020,159	272–274	Other credit accounts	3,096,101	11,731,013
9,731,023				
42,464,832				48,378,856

Previous year	Account	Item		Current year
23,639,965	121–122	Projects under construction . .		26,245,128
2,794,240	131–136	Inventories	3,995,515	
3,764,777	161, 173	Receivables	4,936,776	
388	181–183	Cash	851	8,933,142
30,199,370				
1,933,572		Accumulated losses & losses from revaluation		1,933,572
42,464,832				48,378,857

EXHIBIT 2.3B *Alnaser Company PROFIT AND LOSS ACCOUNT (For the Year Ended June 30, 1971)*

1969–1970 Egyptian Pounds	Uniform Account No.		Egyptian Pounds	Egyptian Pounds
857,822		Gross production & trading profit		1,790,077
		Transferred Revenues		
256,121	441	Interest earned . .		
6,437	442	Rents earned	3,903	
23,091	444	Prior years' revenues	28,106	
	445	Fines earned	66	
915	446	Other revenues . .	413	
102,316	447	Differences between assumed rents for depreciable assets and their depreciation	100,638	
370,609	448	Difference in interest	288,843	421,969
1,617,311				2,212,046

1969–1970 Egyptian Pounds	Uniform Account No.		Egyptian Pounds	Egyptian Pounds
		Administrative & Financing Expenses		
54,149	831	Wages	89,590	
44,557	832	Raw materials & supplies used . .	1,261	
14,469	833	Services acquired	8,958	
630,795	835	Current transferred expenses	653,894	753,703
743,970				
		Current Transfer		
252	361	Gifts.	20	
101	362	Contributions to others.		
	363	Fines	1,969	
99,592	365	Prior years' expenses	32,666	
454,819	367	Additional allowance for depreciation	1,342,591	1,377,246
554,764				
318,577	228	Profits for the period		81,097
1,617,311				2,212,046

EXHIBIT 2.3C *Alnaser Company CURRENT OPERATIONS ACCOUNT (For the Year Ended June 30, 1971)*

1969–1970 Egyptian Pounds	*Uniform Account No.*		*Egyptian Pounds*	*Egyptian Pounds*
		Value of Production & Services		
		Production at selling price:		
7,021,300	411	Net sales of finished goods . . .	8,518,483	
(197,271)	412	Cost of the difference between beginning and ending finished goods	382,506	

1969–1970 Egyptian Pounds	*Uniform Account No.*		*Egyptian Pounds*	*Egyptian Pounds*
		Wages		
429,201	311	Monetary wages	452,158	
100,865	312, 313	Nonmonetary wages.	107,013	559,171
530,066				
		General Expenditures		
4,568,221	32	Raw materials & supplies used . .	5,633,766	
174,615	33	Services acquired	178,586	
179,694	34	Finished goods purchased for sale		5,812,352
4,922,530				
		Current Transferred Expenditures		
363,743	3511	Custom duties . . .	371,939	
9,399	3514	Other taxes (e.g., tax on franchises)	4,348	376,287
373,142				

EXHIBIT 2.3C (continued) *Alnaser Company CURRENT OPERATIONS ACCOUNT (For the Year Ended June 30, 1971)*

1969–1970 Egyptian Pounds	*Uniform Account No.*		*Egyptian Pounds*	*Egyptian Pounds*
(155,420)	413	Changes in value of the difference between beginning and ending finished goods		
6,668,609		goods	(486,329)	8,414,660
16,711	414	Cost of the difference between beginning and ending work in process	(17,386)	
230	416	Revenues from others.		
28,757	417	Services sold	26,364	8,978
45,698				
		Finished Goods Purchased for Sale		
240,455	4181	Net sales.	—	
(31,278)	4182	Cost of the difference between beginning and		

1969–1970 Egyptian Pounds	*Uniform Account No.*		*Egyptian Pounds*	*Egyptian Pounds*
		Depreciation		
60,181	3522	Bldg., constructions & roads . .	76,421	
315,958	3523	Equipment	347,857	
25,514	3524	Cars	26,126	
3,422	3525	Tools	4,988	
3,308	3526	Furniture.	3,793	
	3528	Deferred revenue expenditure . . .	32,774	491,959
408,383				
11,639	353	Rent expense	9,991	
102,316	354	Difference between assumed rents for depreciable assets and their depreciations . . .	100,638	110,629
113,955				
		Interest Expenses		
204,227	355	Local interest . . .	197,353	
42,360	356	Foreign interest . .	36,999	
370,609	357	Difference in interest	288,843	523,195
616,976				
(155,420)	358	Changes in value		

		ending finished goods		
(6,053)	4183	Changes in value of goods purchased for sale on hand		
203,124				
6,917,431				8,423,638
113,852		Income from normal operations		1,036,374
		Transferred Revenues		
256,121	441	Interest earned ..		
6,437	442	Rents earned	3,903	
23,091	444	Prior years' revenues	28,106	
	445	Fines earned	66	
915	446	Other revenues ..	413	
102,316	447	Difference between assumed rents for depreciable assets and their depreciations ...	100,638	
370,609	448	Difference in interest	288,843	421,969
759,489				
873,341				1,458,343

		goods produced on hand		(486,329)
(6,053)	359	Changes in value of goods purchased for sale on hand		—
113,852		Income from normal operations		1,036,374
6,917,431				8,423,638
		Current Transfers		
252	361	Gifts...........	20	
101	362	Contributions to others........	—	
	363	Fines	1,969	
99,592	365	Prior years' expenses	32,666	
454,819	367	Additional allowance for depreciation	1,342,591	1,377,246
554,764				
318,577	228	Profits for the period		81,097
873,341				1,458,343

EXHIBIT 2.3D *Alnaser Company PRODUCTION AND TRADING ACCOUNT (For the Year Ended June 30, 1971)*

1969–1970 Egyptian Pounds	Uniform Account No.		Egyptian Pounds	Egyptian Pounds
16,712	414	Cost of the differences between beginning and ending work in process	(17,386)	(17,386)
6,010,388		Cost of production		7,119,794
6,027,100				7,102,408

1969–1970 Egyptian Pounds	Uniform Account No.		Egyptian Pounds	Egyptian Pounds
		Production Centers		
198,336	531	Wages	225,751	
4,425,814	532	Raw materials & supplies used . .	5,384,379	
58,330	533	Services acquired	109,010	
811,923	535	Current transferred expenses	759,724	6,478,864
5,494,403				
		Service Centers		
271,988	631	Wages	238,465	
92,716	632	Raw materials & supplies used . .	239,193	
100,043	633	Services acquired	58,698	
67,950	635	Current transferred expenses	87,188	623,544
532,697				
6,027,100				7,102,408
6,010,388		Cost of production		7,119,794
179,694	534	Finished goods purchased for sale		

Prior year	Account	*Value of Production & Services*		
		Production at selling price:		
7,021,300	411	Net sales of finished goods . . .	8,518,483	
(197,271)	412	Cost of the difference between beginning and ending finished goods . . .	382,506	
(155,420)	413	Changes in value of the difference between beginning and ending finished goods . . .	(486,329)	
6,668,809				8,414,660
230	416	Revenues from others.		
28,757	417	Services sold	26,364	26,364
		Finished Goods Purchased for Sale		
240,456	4181	Net sales.	—	
(31,278)	4182	Cost of the difference between beginning and ending finished goods	—	

Prior year	Account			
(155,420)	538	Changes in value of finished goods produced on hand	(486,329)	
(6,053)	539	Difference in value of goods purchased for sale on hand. . .		(486,329)
18,221				
872,112		Gross production profit		1,807,559

EXHIBIT 2.3D (continued) *Alnaser Company PRODUCTION AND TRADING ACCOUNT (For the Year Ended June 30, 1971)*

1969–1970 Egyptian Pounds	*Uniform Account No.*		*Egyptian Pounds*	*Egyptian Pounds*	*1969–1970 Egyptian Pounds*	*Uniform Account No.*		*Egyptian Pounds*	*Egyptian Pounds*
(6,053)	4183	Changes in value of goods purchased for sale on hand	—						
6,900,721				8,441,024	6,900,721				8,441,024
872,112		Gross production profit		1,807,559			*Marketing Centers*		
					5,594	731	Wages	5,364	
					5,135	732	Raw materials & supplies used ..	8,934	
					1,771	733	Services acquired	1,920	
					1,790	735	Current transferred expenses	1,264	17,482
					14,290				
					857,822		Gross production & trading profit		1,790,077
872,112				1,807,559	872,112				1,807,559

EXHIBIT 2.3E *Alnaser Company VALUE–ADDED STATEMENT (For the Year Ended June 30, 1971)*

1969–1970 Egyptian Pounds	*Uniform Account No.*	*Value of Production and Services at Selling Price*	*Budgeted Egyptian Pounds*	*Actual Egyptian Pounds*
			(in thousands of pounds)	
		Production at selling price:		
7,021	411	Net sales of finished goods	7,308	8,518
(197)	412	Cost of the difference between beginning and ending finished goods	28	383
(155)	413	Changes in value of finished goods produced on hand	2	(486)
17	414	Cost of the difference between beginning and ending work in process	12	(17)
29	417	Services sold	19	26
		Finished goods purchased for sale:		
240	4181	Net sales	—	—
(31)	4182	Cost of the difference between beginning and ending finished goods	—	—
(6)	4183	Changes in value of goods purchased for sale on hand	—	—
6,918		Total	7,369	8,424
(180)	34	Less: Finished goods purchased for sale	—	—
6,738		Value of production and services at selling price	7,369	8,424

EXHIBIT 2.3E (continued) *Alnaser Company VALUE-ADDED STATEMENT (For the Year Ended June 30, 1971)*

1969–1970 Egyptian Pounds	*Uniform Account No.*	*Value of Production and Services at Selling Price*	*Budgeted Egyptian Pounds*	*Actual Egyptian Pounds*
			(in thousands of pounds)	
		Less:		
(364)	3511	Custom duties	(402)	(372)
(9)	3514	Other taxes	(5)	(4)
6,365		Value of production and services at factors of production costs	6,962	8,048
		Less:		
(4,568)	32	Raw materials and supplies used	(6,535)	(5,634)
(175)	33	Services acquired	(240)	(178)
(408)	3522–3528	Depreciation	(575)	(492)
1,214		Net value-added at factors of production costs	(388)	1,744
		Distribution of Value-Added:		
530	311–313	Wages	601	559
114	353–354	Rents	114	111
617	355–357	Interest	916	523
(155)	358	Changes in value of finished goods produced on hand	2	(486)
(6)	4183	Changes in value of goods purchased for sale on hand	—	—
144		Income from normal operations	(2,021)	1,037
1,214			(388)	1,744

SOURCE: *The Accounting Review*, Vol. 46, Supplement 1976, pp. 82–89.

EXHIBIT 2–4 *Standards and Exposure Drafts of the IASC as of March 1983*

	Definitive Standards
IAS–1	Disclosure of Accounting Policies
IAS–2	Valuation and Presentation of Inventories in the Context of the Historical Cost System
IAS–3	Consolidated Financial Statements
IAS–4	Depreciation Accounting
IAS–5	Information to be Disclosed in Financial Statements
IAS–6	Accounting Responses to Changing Prices
IAS–7	Statement of Changes in Financial Position
IAS–8	Unusual and Prior Period Items and Changes in Accounting Policies
IAS–9	Accounting for Research and Development Activities
IAS–10	Contingencies and Events Occurring After the Balance Sheet Data
IAS–11	Accounting for Construction Contracts
IAS–12	Accounting for Taxes on Income
IAS–13	Presentation of Current Assets and Liabilities
IAS–14	Reporting Financial Information by Segment
IAS–15	Information for Reflecting the Effects of Changing Prices
IAS–16	Accounting for Property, Plant, and Equipment
IAS–17	Accounting for Leases
IAS–18	Revenue Recognition
IAS–19	Accounting for Retirement Benefits in the Financial Statements of Employers
	Exposure Drafts Outstanding
E–21	Accounting for Government Grants and Disclosure of Government Assistance
E–22	Accounting for Business Combinations
E–23	Accounting for the Effects of Changes in Foreign Exchange Rates
E–24	Capitalization of Borrowing Costs
E–25	Disclosure of Related Party Transactions

national accounting standards to the IASC. The IFAC's twelve-point program is listed in Exhibit 2.5.

The current membership of the IFAC consists of 83 professional accounting organizations from 62 countries. To date, IFAC's International Auditing Practices Committee has issued twelve definitive International Auditing Guidelines and seven Exposure Drafts. (For a list of these, see Exhibit 7.2 in Chapter 7, p. 201.) In addition, IFAC's Ethics Committee issued in 1980 its first definitive standard entitled "Guideline on Professional Ethics for the Accounting Profession," as well

EXHIBIT 2.5 *IFAC's Twelve-Point Program*

1. Develop statements that would serve as guidelines for international auditing practices.
2. Establish a suggested minimum code of ethics to which it is hoped that member bodies would subscribe and which could be further refined as appropriate.
3. Determine the requirements and develop programs for the professional education and training of accountants.
4. Evaluate, develop, and report on financial management and other management accounting techniques and procedures.
5. Collect, analyze, research, and disseminate information on the management of public accounting practices to assist practitioners in conducting their practices more effectively.
6. Undertake other studies of value to accountants such as, possibly, a study of the legal liability of auditors.
7. Foster close relations with users of financial statements, including preparers, trade unions, financial institutions, industry, governments, and others.
8. Maintain close relations with regional bodies and explore the potential for establishing other regional bodies as well as for assisting in their organization and development, as appropriate. Assign appropriate projects to existing regional bodies.
9. Establish regular communication among the members of IFAC and with other interested organizations through the medium of a newsletter.
10. Organize and promote the exchange of technical information, educational materials, and professional publications and other literature emanating from member bodies.
11. Organize and conduct an international Congress of Accountants approximately every five years.
12. Seek to expand the membership of the IFAC.

SOURCE: Joseph P. Cummings and Michael N. Chetkovich, "World Accounting Enters a New Era," *The Journal of Accountancy*, 145, April 1978, p. 52. Copyright © 1978 by the American Institute of Certified Public Accountants, Inc.

as a "Statement of Guidance" dealing with advertising, publicity, solicitation, and professional competence.

Other Organizations

The United Nations, through its Commission and Center on Transnational Reporting Corporations, has been actively involved in gathering information on multinational activities and is moving toward establishing international accounting standards, with particular emphasis on increased disclosure in financial statements. Many of these efforts have concerned social responsibility reporting issues, but these activities have not yet materialized in the form of a definitive UN pronouncement.

Another body, the Organization for Economic Cooperation and Development (OECD) is an intergovernmental entity of twenty-four countries, established in December 1960 to "achieve the highest sustainable economic growth and employment and a rising standard of living in member countries while maintaining financial stability and, thus, to contribute to the world economy." The OECD in 1976 proposed a code of conduct for multinational enterprises, dealing in part with accounting matters (that is, financial disclosure).

In addition to the international agencies and bodies, there are many regional organizations dealing with accounting matters, such as the Inter-American Accounting Association (IAA), the Conference of Asian and Pacific Accountants (CAPA), the *Union Europèene des Experts Comptables Economiques et Financiers*, or "Union of European Accountants" (UEC), and the European Economic Community (EEC). These organizations have succeeded in generating some interest in the establishment of international accounting standards.

As a pioneer regional organization, the EEC was established by the Treaty of Rome on March 25, 1957, to promote full freedom in the movement of goods and labor between member countries (Belgium, Denmark, France, Greece, Ireland, Italy, Luxembourg, the Netherlands, the United Kingdom, and West Germany). Therefore, one of the objectives of the EEC has been the creation of a unified business environment, involving the harmonization of company laws and taxation, and the creation of a community capital market. As a by-product of this cooperation, the EEC issued directives for the harmonization of accounting standards for its members. The harmonized system of accounts that resulted is related to (1) the presentation of financial statements for enterprises in the EEC, (2) the method of valuation of assets, (3) the utilization of the "true and fair" presentation concept, and (4) the disclosure requirement (that is, the Fourth Directive, which was officially adopted by the Council of Ministers of the EEC on July 24, 1978). The main objectives of the Fourth Directive are: (1) to coordinate the various national laws governing the publication, presentation, and content of financial statements; (2) to establish throughout the EEC minimum requirements for the disclosure of financial information by companies; (3) to establish the underlying principle that financial statements should give a "true and fair view" of a company's financial position and the results of its operations; and (4) to protect the interests of such third parties as employees, trade unions, governmental bodies, and creditors.

Upon the publication of the directives of the EEC, member countries have two years to change their national laws to adhere to the directives. However, the provisions of the directives are usually flexible enough to permit member countries to have discretionary power as to how the directives are to be incorporated into national laws. Since different environments demand the use of different accounting systems, this has proven to be a wise policy.

Finally, local organizations, such as the International Section of the American Accounting Association, have also been promoting interest in international accounting. The International Section of the AAA represents the attempt of the academic community to improve communications between professionals in different countries and to establish international accounting standards.

STUDY QUESTIONS FOR CHAPTER 2

1. Discuss the following and give examples:

   Accounting regulations have long been recognized in most countries as a means of securing the reliability of accounting reports. By harmonizing the way in which reports are prepared, the accounting regulations can ensure that they are of real value to their users.

2. Why do accounting regulations vary from one environment to another?
3. Compare accounting policy formulation between Latin American countries and those of continental Europe, and state the reasons for any differences.
4. What are the essential features that distinguish accounting requirements in Europe from those of Anglo-America?
5. What is the difference between accounting regulations in the United Kingdom and in the United States?
6. There has been dissatisfaction from both within and without the accounting profession as to the present processes of formulating accounting standards and procedures. What would you propose?

7. What are the chances for increased governmental legislation of accounting matters in the U.S.?
8. Who should formulate accounting policies in different environments—the accounting profession, the government, or both?
9. Briefly discuss the efforts, successes, and failures of the major regional and international organizations trying to establish international accounting standards.
10. What impact does nationalism have on the harmonization of accounting standards?

ADDITIONAL REFERENCES

1. AlHashim, Dhia D. "Accounting Control through Purpose Uniformity: An International Perspective." *International Journal of Accounting*, Spring 1973.
2. AlHashim, Dhia D. "Regulation of Financial Accounting: An International Perspective." *International Journal of Accounting*, Fall 1980.
3. AlHashim, Dhia D. and Garner S. Paul. "Postulates for Localized Uniformity in Accounting." *Abacus*, June 1973.
4. Arpan, Jeffrey, and Radebaugh, Lee. *International Accounting and Multinational Enterprises*. Boston: Warren, Gorham, and Lamont, 1981, Chapter 3.
5. Arthur Andersen & Co. *Accounting Standards for Enterprises Throughout the World*. Chicago, Illinois: Arthur Andersen & Co., 1974.
6. Benston, George J. "Accounting Standards in the United States and the United Kingdom: Their Nature, Causes and Consequences." *Vanderbilt Law Review*, January 1975.
7. Grady, Paul. *Inventory of Generally Accepted Accounting Principles for Business Enterprises*. Accounting Research Study No. 7. New York: AICPA, 1965.
8. Higgins, Thomas S., and Bevis, Herman. "Generally Accepted Accounting Principles—Their Definition and Authority." *The New York Certified Public Accountant*, February 1964.
9. Horngren, Charles T. "Accounting Principles: Private or Public?" *Journal of Accountancy*, May 1972.
10. May, Robert G., and Sundem, Gary L. "Research for Accounting Policy: An Overview." *Accounting Review*, October 1976.

11. Sprouse, Robert T., and Moonitz, Maurice. *A Tentative Set of Broad Accounting Principles for Business Enterprises.* Accounting Research Study No. 3. New York: AICPA, 1962.

12. Zeff, Stephen A. *Forging Accounting Principles in Five Countries: A History and an Analysis of Trends.* Champaign, Illinois: Stipes Publishing Company, 1971.

Chapter 3

Income Determination and Financial Analysis

Anyone who owns or invests in a company is naturally concerned with its financial success. Also the firm's creditors, employees, suppliers, customers, and government each have a certain stake in the company's financial well being. To learn how a company is doing financially, certain information is required—the types of information generally contained in a firm's financial statements: the income statement, the balance sheet, and the flow of funds statement. All of these statements, in turn, rely on specific methods of valuation—assigning a monetary value, such as dollars, to economic transactions, revenues and expenses, and to units such as assets and liabilities. Finally, making sense of all these statements requires some analytical techniques and a process customarily referred to as financial analysis.

The purpose of this chapter is to show how income determination and valuation procedures differ among countries, the problems that these differences pose for financial analysis in general, and how they complicate life for a multinational enterprise's accounting staff.

VALUATION AND INCOME DETERMINATION

While profit may not be the only or even most important goal for all businesses, it is certainly an important goal for most—if nothing else, as a means to achieve other objectives of the firm. Therefore, the determination of income is also an important activity for a firm, an activity generally in the hands and pencils, if you will, of accountants.

In a conceptual sense, the determination of income is a fairly straightforward process. The expenses incurred in producing and selling a product should be subtracted from the revenues the product generates. Revenues, in the complete sense of the word, include not only the income from the sales of a company's products, but other income received from the use of the company's assets, such as a company's interest on savings accounts or other returns on investments. Expenses, in the broad sense, include labor, materials, facilities, and activities such as research and development, advertising, and administration. Yet while the basic income determination process is thus essentially the same for all firms, the underlying valuation processes can and do differ drastically around the world. The relationship of valuation to income determination can be illustrated by considering inventories.

In the manufacturing process, inventories are accumulated, used up, and occasionally left over. Typically, to determine income, monetary values must be assigned to beginning and ending inventory in order to determine the value of inventory used in the manufacture of the product. This is an important element of the income determination process, and is essentially the same for all firms in all countries. However, the inventory may be valued using different methods such as LIFO, FIFO, replacement cost, direct labor cost, or weighted average cost, to name just a few. This is the valuation process. And as any basic accounting textbook shows, different methods of valuing inventory result in different amounts of income for the firm. For example, in inflationary periods using LIFO or replacement cost valuation methods result in a lower income than using the FIFO method does. Hence, there is a direct relationship between income determination and the valuation process.

The relationship described for inventory valuation and income determination extends to the valuation of the firm's every asset and liability. How fixed assets are valued and depreciated, how research and development activities are valued and either expensed or amortized, and how liabilities (actually incurred or contingent) are valued all affect how income and profit are ultimately determined. Yet, the valuation process involves many different methods in different countries, and sometimes even within the same country. We will now take a look at this variety.

Valuation Principles and Procedures[1]

Fixed Assets

Let us first consider the valuation of fixed assets. In Colombia, Germany, Greece, Japan, Kenya, Spain, and the United States, fixed assets are valued at cost of acquisition or construction, less accumulated depreciation. In 29 other countries, this procedure is followed by a majority of firms. However, in Argentina, Bolivia, Brazil, Peru, Uraguay and Venezuela, it is done only by a minority of firms. And in Chile, this procedure is not permitted—fixed assets, by law, must be written up at least annually by applying indices to account for price level changes. The differences in the approach to the valuation of fixed assets are heavily influenced by relative rates of inflation in the various countries, that is, by the departures from historical cost in hyperinflationary situations.

In the United States and nine other countries including Japan, Germany, and Switzerland, valuing fixed assets at their appraised values is not permitted, but in France, it is required by law. In thirty other countries it is done by a minority of firms. Finally, many countries have revaluation reserves—surpluses arising on the revaluation of assets—an account and accounting procedure not applicable in the United States. In at least 26 countries, these revaluation reserves are available for stock dividends, but in four other countries, they are not available for this purpose by law. And while most countries who permit such reserves do not allow them to be used for cash dividends, in at least five countries, including Italy and South Africa, they can be used for this purpose.

---

[1]The information about specific country practices for this section draws heavily on the material contained in Price Waterhouse's publication, *Accounting Principles and Reporting Practices: A Survey in 46 Countries*, 1975.

Leases

In terms of leases, U.S. GAAP requires leases to be capitalized (treated as an installment purchase) when the substance of the arrangement transfers the usual risks and rewards of ownership from the lessor to the lessee, a procedure also required in Mexico. However, this procedure is followed by a majority of firms in only thirteen other countries, is not permitted in France, and is not found (although it is not prohibited) in the practices of 21 other countries, mostly developing nations.

Depreciation

In terms of depreciation, only the United States and five other countries require charges to income for depreciation based on the normal life of an asset to be adjusted for early economic obsolescence. And only the United States, Canada, Japan, Mexico, and Ireland require that depreciation be based on the cost of the asset less the estimated salvage value at the end of its estimated useful life. In contrast, this is not done in France, Italy, Peru, or Paraguay, and is a practice of only a minority of firms in 21 other countries.

The most common practice throughout the world is to disregard the estimated salvage value in determining depreciation. In addition, in more than 20 countries the methods and rates of depreciation used for financial statement purposes adhere strictly to tax requirements—a procedure not practiced in the United States, and not permitted in the United Kingdom. Finally, an overconservative stance taken by excessively charging for the depreciation of fixed assets is evident in a majority of Swiss, French, Swedish, Belgian, Brazilian, and Danish firms, and in a minority of the firms of 21 other countries. However, this overconservative procedure is not permitted in nine countries, including the United Kingdom and the Netherlands, and is not practiced in nine others. In the United States, it is followed only by a minority of firms.

Inventory

Regarding inventory valuation, a majority of firms in Colombia and Spain never adjust inventories to the lower market value. But in 17 other countries, including the United States and the United Kingdom, adjusting to the lower market values is required. In addition, while the United Kingdom, France, Germany, Japan, and 12 other countries do not permit the practice of undisclosed undervaluations of inventories, this practice is followed by a majority of firms in Denmark, Italy, Spain, and Switzerland, and by a minority of firms in 14 other countries, including the United States. Finally, in the United States and most countries, the common practice is to include in the cost of inventory direct material and labor, and all variable and fixed manufacturing overheads (including depreciation) evaluated at the level of normal operating capacity. However, Chile requires that only prime costs—that is, direct labor and direct materials—be included in the cost of inventory, a procedure not permitted in the United States, the United Kingdom, Japan, Canada, Mexico, or Ireland.

Long Term Debt

The valuation principles and procedures for long term debt also vary considerably among countries. For example, the United States and three other countries do not permit the discount on a long term debt issue to be written off in the year in which it occurs. However, this procedure is practiced by a majority of firms in five other countries, including the United Kingdom and Sweden, and by a minority of firms in 20 other countries, including Japan, Germany, and Canada. On the other hand, the most commonly followed procedure in the United States, amortizing the discount over the term of the debt by the interest method, is followed by a majority of firms in only 11 other countries, is not practiced in 15 countries, and is not permitted at all in France.

Share Valuation

Regarding the valuation of the shares of a company's own stock it reacquires, 9 countries require that they be valued at cost and shown as a reduction of shareholder's equity, and in 9 countries, including the United States, this procedure is followed by a majority of firms. However, the same procedure is not allowed in 15 countries, including Germany, Japan, Mexico, and South Africa. In addition, the United States is virtually alone in its valuation treatment of dividends satisfied by stock issues (share distributions). In most of the world, share distributions are recorded at par value when there is no cash option, a practice not permitted in the U.S. because the U.S. requires the valuation of share distributions of less than 20% at the greater of either the quoted market or another current value.

Research and Development

The United States also almost stands alone in its treatment of research and development costs in cases where the work and related expenditures are clearly identifiable and where there are grounds for accepting that such costs will be covered by some future revenue. These costs are deferred and amortized by a majority or half of the firms in twenty countries, and by a minority of firms in 17 countries. In the United States and Germany, however, this practice is not permitted—all R and D costs must be expensed as incurred.

The Matching Concept

The assignment of values to income statement and balance sheet items is only one aspect of income determination. An equally important aspect is determining which expenses are to be associated, assigned, or matched to which revenues. In the United States and most other countries, a "matching concept" exists, meaning expenses associated with a particular sale are "matched" with that sale, regardless of when those expenses were actually paid. In some countries, however, revenues and expenses are assigned to a specific year, without regard to their actual relationship to each other. Thus, advertising expenses paid at the end of a company's fiscal year are recorded in that year even if the product is not sold until the following year. This is often referred to as the "cash" method. Thus, the method of determining when expenses and revenues are recognized and realized also affects income determination.

The Use of Reserves

Still another major aspect of income determination involves the use of various reserves. In the most general sense, reserves are used to provide for contingencies. The valuation of such reserves—which can effectively increase or decrease their amount—affects income. For example, in the United States there are "allowances for bad debts" (a kind of reserve) to recognize and prepare for the possibility that not all customers will pay in full for what they have purchased on credit from the company. The allowance for bad debts is an attempt to match expected losses from sales against the revenue from those sales. Other reserves in the United States take the form of "appropriated retained earnings"—retained earnings which cannot be distributed to shareholders for various reasons, such as the potential expense of losing a legal suit.

While there is nothing unusual about these kinds of reserves, there is something unusual about the extent and the kind of roles reserves play in countries other than the United States. In most cases, the use of reserves is far more extensive in other countries. In fact, the establishment of legal or statutory reserves is required by law in more than thirty countries. For example, Swiss balance sheets typically have four major categories of reserves: statutory, relief work, free, and special. For the Swiss company CIBA-GEIGY, in 1973 the combined value of these reserves amounted to over 1.5 billion Swiss francs, compared to an issued capital of only slightly more than 464 million Swiss francs. Thus, the reserves comprised nearly 80% of the company's total equity at the end of the year, and equalled nearly 40% of the value of its total assets. For the German based B.A.S.F. company, in 1973 its statutory reserves, free reserves, special reserves, and general reserves for accounts receivable totalled over 2.1 billion deutschmarks, representing over 50% of its total equity and equal in value to 20% of its total assets. As a final example, the Egyptian-based Alnaser company's combined reserves (appropriations of equity) and numerous "allowances" (including allowances for disputed taxes) in 1971 totalled over 7.8 million Egyptian pounds, or 40% of its total capital.

In many countries, movements of funds into and out of reserves directly affects reported and taxable income. A firm that has a highly profitable year can and often must by law place a certain portion of that income into a reserve account, and thereby *exclude* that portion from its reported and/or taxable income for the period. In essence, then, the firm *understates* its actual income. In other cases, if a firm did not have a particularly profitable year but, for whatever reason, wants to report a higher level of income, it can take money out of a previously established reserve and add this amount to the reported income for the period—in essence *overstating* its actual income. The use of reserves for these purposes results in what is called "income smoothing": smoothing or leveling the actual income to an acceptable or desirable amount. The use of general reserves to transfer income between periods is done by a majority of firms in Switzerland, about half the firms in Italy, and exists as a practice in at least 12 other countries. In addition, reserves are increased or decreased without disclosing the amounts charged or credited to them (or the reasons therefore) by a majority of firms in Brazil,

Italy, Switzerland, Paraguay, and Spain, and by a minority of firms in 15 other countries, including France, Belgium, Sweden, and Chile.

Clearly, in countries where income smoothing is practiced to a significant degree, the income statements of firms are less meaningful for financial analysis, particularly when the movements of funds into and out of reserves are not disclosed. In fact, in a number of countries the actual existence of reserves is not even disclosed. These are called "hidden" or "silent" reserves.

Off-Balance Sheet Accounting

Hidden reserves are just one form of the kind of accounting referred to as "off-balance sheet" accounting, a method where various financial transactions or contingencies do not appear on the formal records or financial statements of the firm. Expenses related to the use of illegal workers, or revenues resulting from illegal activities—or even legal activities—are a few examples. Unlike silent reserves, however, most forms of off-balance sheet accounting tend to be illegal, that is, they are purposely done to cheat the government out of taxes, to evade government policies, or to mislead competitors, investors, or creditors.

Off-balance sheet accounting tends to flourish in countries where accounting rules are imprecise or lack sophistication, or where professional standards and ethics are not very high. However, its use is not unknown in the United States, despite the general perception that the U.S. accounting system is highly advanced—*and* despite the perception that American accountants and managers maintain relatively high ethical standards. For example, the investigations of the congressional "Watergate" committee in the 1970s revealed numerous off-balance sheet accounting practices. Some of the largest companies in the United States practiced such malfeasance in order to make illegal political contributions both inside and outside the United States. Such "corrupt practices" are discussed more in Chapter 7. The major point of our discussion here of off-balance sheet accounting is to point out that it can and does significantly affect both income determination and the reliability or usefulness of financial statements.

FINANCIAL ANALYSIS

Having looked at the variations in the methods of income determination, we will now examine financial analysis. As we know, accounting exists primarily to provide useful information for decision-making purposes to people both inside and outside the firm. The study of financial analysis helps these people to understand the meaning of the accounting data they see. That is, financial analysis is an interpretive activity. When they are performing a financial analysis, people are interpreting a mass of information and dollar amounts that would be difficult to understand simply viewed as a whole.

While one could gain some understanding of a firm's activities, progress, and well-being by analyzing the written narratives in company documents such as the annual reports, such narratives do not provide a complete picture. The complete picture can only be obtained by properly analyzing the firm's financial records and statements. To accomplish this, one must first obtain as complete a set of financial information about the firm as possible. Next, a series of financial analysis procedures should be undertaken, and the results should be analyzed in both absolute and comparative terms. The comparative aspects involve comparisons to previous years, to other firms in the industry, and to industry averages.

Financial Ratio Analysis

A widely accepted method of financial analysis is ratio analysis: a comparison of two related pieces of information about a firm. The ratio is derived from the common fraction of the two in percentage form, such as the debt-to-equity ratio: total debt divided by stockholders' equity.

While there are literally hundreds of ratios that could be calculated, certain ratios are more applicable and useful than others, depending on the interests of the person doing the analysis. For example, investors in common stocks are more concerned with the long-term aspects of a company, and focus on its earnings records. Net income is a proxy for operating efficiency, and provides some indication as to whether a common stock is a good investment. Therefore, these investors are typically interested in earnings per share, the price earnings ratio, the dividend payout ratio, divided yields, the return on equity or sales, and debt-to-equity ratios.

On the other hand, short-term creditors are typically interested in the ability of the firm to generate sufficient cash to pay current liabilities and still have enough money left over to meet current operating needs. As a result, short-term creditors focus more on a company's cash position and its near cash resources (or current assets) in relation to its short-term liabilities. Thus they look more closely at liquidity ratios such as the current ratio and the "acid-test" or quick ratio, and at the ratios concerning the movement of current assets, such as receivables turnover, inventory turnover, and the average number of days to collect receivables.

Finally, long-term creditors are mainly interested in the ability of a firm to meet the interest payments over the life of a loan and to repay the principal of the loan at maturity. Therefore, the firm's debt-to-equity ratio is an important consideration, as well as the number of times the interest has been earned.

Shortcomings of Ratio Analysis

When properly used, ratio analyses can be very helpful in assessing a company's financial operations and well-being. However, there are many inherent weaknesses. Johnson and Gentry[2] list the following:

> 1. By the time the outsider has obtained financial statements, the data are out of date.
>
> 2. Ratio analysis uses historical data, and there is some question as to whether historical data can provide a relevant basis for making predictions.
>
> 3. Diverse accounting treatments of inventory, depreciation, and capitalization versus expensing of outlays and the like, make meaningful comparisons of companies via ratio analysis difficult.
>
> 4. Ratio analysis by itself overlooks the dynamic aspects of the flow of resources through a firm, [even though determining the resource flow] is . . . helpful in evaluating management efficiency.
>
> 5. Ratio analysis normally uses financial data that are not adjusted for changes in the level of general prices, which can distort the analysis.
>
> 6. There has been a tendency to develop a multiplicity of ratios, some of which have little or no significance. If two dollar amounts have little or no significance in relation to each other, a ratio expression of their relation is no more significant. For instance, it is claimed by some that the ratio of current assets to long-term debt is meaningful, but it is difficult to see why.
>
> 7. [Certain] ratios . . . can give misleading results. For example, the turnover of working capital is often regarded as a very significant ratio

[2]Glenn L. Johnson, James A. Gentry, Jr., *Finney and Miller's Principles of Accounting*, 8th ed., © 1980, pp. 679–680. Reprinted by permission of Prentice-Hall, Inc., Englewood Cliffs, N.J.

> (net sales divided by the working capital). An increase in the ratio is usually interpreted as desirable. But an increase in turnover may be caused by either an increase in sales or a decrease in the working capital. An increase in working-capital turnover caused by a decrease in [the] working capital [itself] may be an undesirable trend.

As the remainder of our discussion will point out, these weaknesses of ratio analysis are more significant when ratio analysis is applied to foreign financial statements. In fact, this is true for other types of financial analysis as well.

Problems in Analyzing Foreign Financial Statements

The Acquisition and Reliability of Information

The first problem in trying to do a financial analysis of a foreign company is acquiring sufficient, reliable information. In the United States, a publicly held firm must publish an annual corporate financial report, and an even more detailed 10-K report if it's listed on a stock exchange, but this is not the case for all the publicly held firms of other countries. In the United States, there are also other sources of financial information about companies, such as Standard and Poors, Moody's Investor Service, Dun and Bradstreet, and Value Line. But most other countries do not have these sources or their equivalent. Finally, in countries where official accounting rules or ethical standards are not followed, companies typically have several sets of "official" books, and many "unofficial" ones. Therefore, getting sufficient and reliable information is not as easy as it may seem.

Language and Terminology

Problems involving language and terminology are a natural obstacle in international accounting and financial analysis. Foreign financial information and reports are usually prepared in the native language of the country where the firm operates. Reading a French firm's reports therefore requires an adequate knowledge of the French language. However, foreign language fluency is not enough, for accounting terminology is very precise, and is not typically learned even by people who thoroughly learn a foreign tongue. In some cases, there may not be any exact equivalent word for a foreign account (such as some "reserve" accounts); or different words may be used for the same account (for example, the British term "turnover" means "sales" in the United

States); or the same word may have a different meaning (for example, short-term debt in one country may mean any debt expected to be repaid within one year, while in another country it may mean a debt expected to be repaid within two or three years, which in the U.S. would typically be classified as a *long-term* debt). Even the term "profit" may have several different definitions, and even within one country. For example, in Egypt, there are several different "profits" to be found in financial statements.

Format

In looking at foreign financial statements, one also notices differences in format. In the United Kingdom, equities are listed on the left side and commence with share capital, with liabilities listed below equities; assets are listed on the right side and commence with fixed asets, progressing down to the most current at the bottom (the reverse of the United States format). France and Germany present assets on the left and liabilities on the right (similar to the U.S.), but also reverse the order within each side as compared to the United States standard: the columns show increasing liquidity in France and Germany, and decreasing liquidity in the U.S.

As shown in Exhibit 3.1A–B, the Germans include among equities the various reserves they are permitted and sometimes required to have by German law, with specific references to particular German accounting regulations. Also, note that their liabilities are divided between those that come due in four years or more, and those that are due within less than four years, unlike the standard U.S. division of one year.

In Italy, even though depreciation is based on cost, the offsetting reserve, accumulated depreciation, is shown on the liability side of the balance sheet. In Brazil, the conventional profit and loss statement combines earned surplus and the income statement, and follows an account form. Gross profit, income from capital not employed in the company's operation, and beginning surplus balance are all shown on the credit side, while expenses and profit distribution are on the debit side. The Egyptians utilize a format that is almost totally different from ones familiar to Americans (see Exhibit 2.3 in Chapter 2).

Still, not every country uses a format different from the one generally used in the United States. Exhibit 3.2A–B shows that the Swiss format is very similar, even though there are some different accounts (primarily reserve accounts in the equity section), some different valuation methods (such as valuing fixed assets at their insured value), and considerably less disclosure. The U.S. format is also followed by Swedish firms, (as shown by Exhibit 3.3A–C), but with significantly greater disclosure than Swiss firms, and, in some instances, greater disclosure than even U.S. firms generally volunteer. (See, for example, some of the explanatory notes reproduced from the Swedish firm's financial statements.)

Currency

Another obvious difference is in the currency used. As is the case with language, foreign financial statements are in terms of their local currency. While ratio analyses are not affected by the particular currency of the financial statement, other aspects of financial analysis can be affected if the exchange value of an escudo, drachma, or riumbini escapes the analyzer's attention. In other words, just how big is a company with sales of one billion escudos?[3]

Different Valuation Methods and Disclosure Practices

But perhaps the worst problems in analyzing foreign financial statements stem from the different valuation methods underlying the statements, many of which were described earlier in this chapter, such as inventory valuation, different adjustments for inflation, and capitalizing versus expensing various items. Unless one understands *how* the numbers were generated, one cannot interpret them correctly. In most cases, foreign financial statements provide few or no explanatory notes to indicate how the statements were prepared. In fact, most foreign financial statements leave undisclosed much of the information typically found in most U.S. and European statements. For example, corporate reports are seldom consolidated, and in some countries, like Colombia, consolidated reports are actually prohibited. In such cases, it is possible to hide losses in unconsolidated affiliates, and to include in the parent company's income statement the profit from intracompany sales which, according to U.S. GAAP, must be eliminated.

Finally, in terms of presentation, in most countries "form" takes precedence over "substance," which is the opposite of U.S. practice. For example, there may be no distinction made between an operating lease

(*Text is continued on page 91.*)

[3]The escudo is the currency of Portugal. One billion escudos in 1980 would have been approximately $20,000,000, translating escudos into U.S. dollars.

EXHIBIT 3.1A *BASF Aktiengesellschaft and Consolidated German Subsidiaries*
CONSOLIDATED BALANCE SHEET at December 31, 1973

Assets	*Dec. 31, 1973 DM*	*Dec. 31, 1972 TDM*
I. Fixed Assets		
A. Tangible and Intangible		
1. Real estate and equivalent rights with office, factory and other buildings	998,396,728	1,002,800
2. Real estate and equivalent rights with residential buildings	166,175,153	149,375
3. Real estate and equivalent rights without buildings	119,647,182	109,031
4. Buildings on land now owned by Group companies and which do not come under (1) or (2)	21,716,630	20,927
5. Machinery, plant and equipment	1,633,030, 689	1,655,656
6. Office equipment	203,198,211	182,541
7. Plant under construction and advances for plant	452,681,958	352,293
8. Concessions, industrial property rights, and similar rights and licenses under such rights	24,296,505	32,292
	3,619,143,056	3,504,915
B. Investments		
1. Affiliated companies	1,969,781,744	1,664,410
2. Securities	958,790	959
3. Loans for a term of at least four years (DM 53,573,584 secured by mortgages on real estate)	100,133,364	97,811
	2,070,873,898	1,763,180
C. Balance Arising from Consolidation	365,579,899	356,003
	6,055,596,853	5,624,098

II. Current Assets		
A. Products on Lease	18,097,320	24,826
B. Inventories	1,185,179,410	1,099,462
C. Uncompleted Contracts	109,029,519	92,819
D. Other Current Assets		
1. Advances paid	19,174,739	19,666
2. Accounts receivable-trade	1,643,673,937	1,409,601
(DM 48,842,626 with a residual term of more than one year)		
3. Bills receivable	78,084,373	123,482
(DM 23,038,656 rediscountable at the Federal Bank)		
4. Checks		45
5. Cash on hand, balances at the Federal Bank and in postal checking accounts	5,700,059	3,884
6. Cash in banks	661,239,177	541,842
(DM 2,826,306 committed)		
7. Securities	107,029,012	97,265
Subtotal items 3–7: cash and cash items	852,052,621	766,518
8. Receivables from affiliates	322,282,849	307,699
9. Receivables resulting from loans granted under or according to		
(a) §89 AktG (corporation law)	24,413,321	36,911
(b) §115 AktG (corporation law)	47,850	60
	24,461,171	36,971
10. Other current assets	118,429,871	82,020
	4,292,381,444	3,839,582
III. Deferred Charges and Prepaid Expenses		
1. Discounts	5,365,367	7,061
2. Others	6,954,853	5,435
	12,320,220	12,496
	10,360,298,517	9,476,176

EXHIBIT 3.1A (continued) *BASF Aktiengesellschaft and Consolidated German Subsidiaries*
CONSOLIDATED BALANCE SHEET at December 31, 1973

Capital and Liabilities		*Dec. 31, 1973 DM*	*Dec. 31, 1972 TDM*
I. Capital Stock		1,526,150,850	1,526,080
Amount paid-in for the capital increase of Jan. 3, 1974		15,000,000	
		1,541,150,850	1,526,080
Conditional capital DM 155,419,650			
II. Surplus Including Consolidated Profit *			
1. Capital surplus		1,354,181,013	1,329,274
2. Earned surplus including consolidated profit		1,055,042,936	906,103
		2,409,223,949	2,235,377
Equity of BASF Aktiengesellschaft and Its Consolidated Subsidiaries:			
* of which: statutory reserve of BASF Aktiengesellschaft	DM 1,159,062,688		
free reserve of BASF Aktiengesellschaft	DM 796,000,000		
consolidated profit	DM 282,637,069		
III. Minority Interests			
1. Capital		139,548,297	136,438
2. Profit		8,543,185	3,644
3. Loss		(10,487,118)	(18,270)
		(1,943,933)	(14,626)
		137,604,364	121,812

IV. Special Reserves	168,983,404	53,903
(according to §§6b and 7c ESIG (income tax law), section 35 EStR (income tax regulations), §74 ESIDV (income tax directive), §1 EHStG (development aid tax law) §1 InvZulG (law on capital expenditures) and §15 BHG (Berlin aid law)		
V. General Reserves for Accounts Receivable	44,537,163	36,587
VI. Accruals		
1. Pension	703,389,989	630,164
2. Others		
a) for taxes	258,124,404	282,826
b) for postponed maintenance work	9,892,500	9,363
c) miscellaneous	627,020,758	492,483
	895,037,662	784,672
	1,598,427,651	1,414,836
VII. Liabilities for a Term of at least Four Years		
1. Bonds (DM 93,100,000 secured by mortgages)	389,504,000	405,604
2. Debentures (DM 91,550,000 secured by mortgages)	234,550,000	266,250
3. Liabilities to banks (DM 183,630,086 secured by mortgages)	1,343,052,864	1,548,250
4. Debts profit levy		408
5. Equalization of Burdens Property Levy	19,465,958	22,625
6. Loans from social and welfare funds (DM 19,971,421 secured by mortgages)	240,896,504	245,240
7. Others (DM 75,421,268 secured by mortgages)	85,668,887	97,269
Items 1–7 comprise DM 1,045,324,941 due within less than four years	2,313,138,223	2,585,646

EXHIBIT 3.1A (continued) *BASF Aktiengesellschaft and Consolidated German Subsidiaries*
CONSOLIDATED BALANCE SHEET at December 31, 1973

VIII. Other Liabilities		
1. Accounts payable-trade	773,749,449	603,671
2. Liabilities from the acceptance and the issue of bills	49,644,615	78,730
3. Liabilities to banks	77,200,177	146,863
4. Advances received	105,767,279	74,727
5. Amounts payable to affiliated companies	659,369,013	210,652
6. Others	479,483,737	383,745
	2,144,214,270	1,498,388
IX. Deferred Income	3,018,643	3,547
	10,360,298,517	9,476,176
1. Liabilities from the issue and endorsement of bills	285,205,661	350,078
2. Liabilities from guarantees	795,655,396	950,618
3. Liabilities from the granting of collateral security for third parties' liabilities	2,826,306	4,623
Present value of the Equalization of Burdens Property Levy	82,749,632	96,432
Quarterly amount of the Equalization of Burdens Property Levy	4,417,853	4,418

EXHIBIT 3.1B *BASF Aktiengesellschaft and Consolidated German Subsidiaries*
STATEMENT OF CONSOLIDATED INCOME for the Year Ended December 31, 1973

	1973			1972		
	DM	*DM*	*DM*	*TDM*	*TDM*	*TDM*
1. Sales		11,412,885,828			9,418,378	
2. Cost of materials (including changes in inventories) and other charges (net) not shown separately below		6,462,158,103	4,950,727,725		5,147,410	4,270,968
			4,950,727,725			4,270,968
3. Income from profit transfer agreements from companies not consolidated		7,130,390			8,031	
4. Income from subsidiaries and affiliates (non-consolidated)		36,156,980			15,281	
5. Income from other investments		2,571,894			2,812	
6. Other interest and similar income		108,275,975			60,411	
7. Valuation adjustments of plant property and investments		2,292,115			10,132	
8. Reversal of accruals		34,409,592			39,345	
9. Other income		101,337,138	292,174,084		125,365	261,377
			5,242,901,809			4,532,345

EXHIBIT 3.1B (continued) *BASF Aktiengesellschaft and Consolidated German Subsidiaries*
STATEMENT OF CONSOLIDATED INCOME for the Year Ended December 31, 1973

	1973			1972		
	DM	*DM*	*DM*	*TDM*	*TDM*	*TDM*
10. Wages and salaries		2,242,197,485			1,885,647	
11. Compulsory social security		292,485,311			232,394	
12. Pensions and assistance		178,705,576			191,072	
13. Depreciation on tangible and intangible fixed assets		712,477,680			693,297	
14. Write-downs and other valuation adjustments of investments		33,087,504			32,077	
15. Interest and similar expenses		265,633,212			240,951	
16. Taxes						
a) on income and property	517,874,080			397,501		
b) others	573,567,645	1,091,441,725		520,573	918,074	
17. Equalization of Burdens Property Levy		16,877,427			16,717	
18. Transfer of losses of affiliates not consolidated		715,427			334	
19. Other mandatory profit distributions under agreement		4,197,963	4,837,819,311		4,137	4,214,700
20. Net income for the year			405,082,499			317,645
21. Loss/profit carryforward			(22,826,264)			17,693
			382,255,234			335,338

22. Transfers to surplus reserves				
a) in the individual financial statements	83,680,334		65,265	
b) in the consolidated financial statements	17,882,764	101,563,098	17,174	82,439
		280,693,136		252,899
23. Minority interests in income	8,543,185		3,644	
24. Minority interests in losses	10,487,118	1,943,933	18,270	14,626
25. Prepaid dividends to third parties		—		800
26. Profit		282,637,069		266,725

The statement of accounts and the report to shareholders follow all legal requirements according to our obligatory examination.

Stuttgart, April 23, 1974
Schitag
Schwäbische Treuhand-Aktiengesellschaft
Wirtschaftsprüfungsgellschaft—
Steuerberatungsgesellschaft
(Certified Public Accountants—
Tax Consultants)
Dr. Frey
Certified Public Accountant
ppa. Dr. Csik
Certified Public Accountant

SOURCE: *The Accounting Review*, Vol. 46, Supplement 1976, pp. 146–148.

EXHIBIT 3.2A *CIBA-GEIGY Limited BALANCE SHEET at December 31, 1973*
(Before Appropriation of Profits)

Assets	*December 31, 1973*		*December 31, 1972*	
	SFr.	*SFr.*	*SFr.*	*SFr.*
Current assets				
Liquid funds, securities				
Cash in hand and with banks	788,747,371		443,392,757	
Securities	294,522,031	1,083,269,402	248,160,934	691,553,691
Accounts receivable				
Customers	288,551,256		308,989,327	
Group companies	444,955,117		323,377,209	
Sundry debtors and prepayments	232,470,497	965,976,870	195,671,483	828,038,019
Stocks		300,389,684		281,966,746
Total current assets		2,349,635,956		1,801,558,456
Long-term assets				
Interests in Group and associated companies		392,177,406		345,643,695
Loans to Group companies and branch establishments		655,280,400		668,688,022
Fixed assets*				
Land	15,000,000		15,000,000	
Industrial buildings	320,150,064		338,636,202	
Office-buildings and dwelling-houses	1		1	
Machinery, equipment and plant	258,566,369	593,716,434	284,745,758	638,381,961
Total long-term assets		1,641,174,240		1,652,713,678
Total assets		3,990,810,196		3,454,272,134
* Insured value of fixed assets	2,208,596,570		1,378,205,020	

Liabilities and Equity	*December 31, 1973*		*December 31, 1972*	
	SFr.	*SFr.*	*SFr.*	*SFr.*
Liabilities				
Accounts payable				
Suppliers	76,911,814		66,402,901	
Group companies	97,267,978		118,657,482	
Banks	—		894,219	
Sundry creditors	380,385,603		305,176,942	
Provisions for commitments and accrued liabilities	1,130,184,244	1,684,749,639	935,695,163	1,426,826,707
Debenture loans				
$3\frac{1}{2}$% Debenture Loan 1959	20,000,000		20,000,000	
$3\frac{3}{4}$% Debenture Loan 1963	50,000,000		50,000,000	
$5\frac{1}{2}$% Option Loan 1973	80,000,000	150,000,000	—	70,000,000
Total liabilities		1,834,749,639		1,496,826,707
Equity				
Issued capital				
Share capital	404,910,000		368,100,000	
Participation certificate capital (authorized: SFr. 87.6m)	59,093,400	464,003,400	46,600,000	414,700,000
Reserves				
Statutory reserve (Swiss Federal Code of Obligations, Article 671)	496,202,423		451,952,323	
Relief work reserve	50,000,000		50,000,000	
Free reserves	309,205,970		297,060,911	
Special reserves and value adjustments	718,297,599	1,573,705,992	638,074,636	1,437,087,870

EXHIBIT 3.2A (continued) *CIBA-GEIGY Limited BALANCE SHEET at December 31, 1973*
(Before Appropriation of Profits)

Liabilities and Equity	*December 31, 1973*		*December 31, 1972*	
	SFr.	*SFr.*	*SFr.*	*SFr.*
Profit and Loss Account				
Net profit for the year	112,939,708		102,120,231	
Balance brought forward from preceding year	5,411,457	118,351,165	3,537,326	105,657,557
Total equity		2,156,060,557		1,957,445,427
Total liabilities and equity		3,990,810,196		3,454,272,134

EXHIBIT 3.2B *CIBA-GEIGY Limited PROFIT AND LOSS ACCOUNT for 1973*

	1973	*1972*
	SFr.	*SFr.*
Revenue		
Sales	2,980,882,001	2,631,425,475
Overhead expenditure recovered	15,263,527	39,667,958
	2,996,145,528	2,671,093,433
Dividends, royalties and interest	230,110,510	287,305,222
Total revenue	3,226,256,038	2,958,398,655
Expenditure		
Raw materials, intermediates, finished products and auxiliaries	1,236,030,459	1,145,728,177
Wages and salaries	699,171,128	648,630,671
Welfare benefits	170,389,848	183,035,789
Other expenditure, including taxes	611,565,044	537,645,169
Depreciation on fixed assets	194,635,482	171,703,939
Depreciation and value adjustments on various assets, and provisions	201,524,369	169,534,679
Total expenditure	3,113,316,330	2,856,278,424
Net Profit	112,939,708	102,120,231

SOURCE: *The Accounting Review*, Vol. 46, Supplement 1976, pp. 173–175

EXHIBIT 3.3A *Gränges AB GROUP BALANCE SHEET, December 31*

	In Thousands of US Dollars 1973	*1972*	*In Millions of Swedish Kronor 1973*
Assets			
Current assets			
Bank balances and cash	$ 39,781	$ 18,381	SKr 181.8
Short-term deposits	70,634	64,836	322.8
	110,415	83,217	504.6
Shares listed (note 7)	15,449	16,390	70.6
Receivables from customers	172,232	134,748	787.1
Other accounts receivable	39,519	27,221	180.6
Inventories (note 8)	234,529	206,433	1,071.8
Total current assets	572,144	468,009	2,614.7
Blocked account for investment fund	22	43	0.1
Fixed assets			
Long-term accounts receivable and investments			
Accounts receivable from allied corporate partnerships	25,711	24,530	117.5
Other accounts receivable	28,031	32,232	128.1
Investments (note 9)	52,713	52,845	240.9
	106,455	109,607	486.5
Property, plant and equipment (note 10)			
Machinery, ships, buildings, etc., at cost	903,982	876,870	4,131.2
Accumulated depreciation	433,873	400,109	1,982.8
	470,109	476,761	2,148.4
Total fixed assets	576,564	586,368	2,634.9
Total assets	$1,148,730	$1,054,420	SKr 5,249.7
Pledged assets (note 11)	$ 273,400	$ 272,600	SKr 1,272.1

EXHIBIT 3.3A (continued)

	In Thousands of US Dollars 1973	*1972*	*In Millions of Swedish Kronor 1973*
Liabilities, Capital and Reserves			
Current liabilities (note 12)			
Accounts payable to suppliers	$ 59,344	$ 50,438	SKr 271.2
Other operating liabilities	118,271	93,698	540.5
	177,615	144,136	811.17
Loans	39,847	35,427	182.1
	217,462	179,563	993.8
Long-term liabilities			
Bond loans and debenture loans (note 13)	109,737	115,689	501.5
Other long-term liabilities (note 13)	91,028	94,726	416.0
	200,765	210,415	917.5
Provisions for pensions (note 14)	62,429	57,243	285.3
	263,194	267,658	1,202.8
Total liabilities	480,656	447,221	2,196.6
Untaxed reserves (note 19)			
Inventory reserve (note 8)	100,323	62,035	458.5
Investment fund	66	66	0.3
Accumulated additional depreciation (note 10)	230,809	213,900	1,054.8
	331,203	276,061	1,513.6
Minority interests in subsidiary companies' capital and reserves (note 15)	11,094	11,444	50.7
Capital and reserves			
Share Capital of Parent Company (5,800,000 common shares with a par value of SKr 100 each)	126,915	126,915	580.0
Reserves not available for dividends (note 16)	46,827	42,429	214.0
Free Reserve Fund of Parent Company	109,409	109,409	500.0
Retained profit (note 17)	42,626	40,941	194.8
Total capital and reserves (note 19)	325,777	319,694	1,488.8
Total liabilities, capital and reserves	$1,143,730	$1,054,420	SKr 5,249.7
Contingent liabilities, etc. (note 18)	$ 35,000	$ 27,300	SKr 124.6

EXHIBIT 3.3B *Gränges AB GROUP PROFIT AND LOSS STATEMENT*

	In Thousands of US Dollars 1973	1972	*In Millions of Swedish Kronor* 1973
Sales to external customers (note 1)	$873,698	$675,558	Skr 3,992.8
Costs of production, selling and administration (note 2)	744,508	616,980	3,402.4
Operating profit before depreciation	129,190	58,578	590.4
Depreciation (note 3)	47,505	43,676	217.1
Operating profit after depreciation (note 4)	81,605	14,902	373.3
Dividends, etc. (note 9)	5,251	5,054	24.0
Interest income	10,744	9,190	49.1
Interest expenditures (note 13)	19,168	18,490	87.6
Profit before taxes and extraordinary items	78,512	10,656	358.8
Current and deferred income taxes (note 5)	35,836	875	164.0
Minority interest in profit after taxes (note 15)	3,567	985	16.3
Equity in undistributed earnings of companies less than 50 percent owned (note 9)	2,845	875	13.0
Profit before extraordinary items	41,904	9,671	191.5

Extraordinary income and expenditures (note 6)	4,201	2,341	19.2
Taxes on extraordinary items (note 5)	2,954	525	13.5
Minority interest in extraordinary items (note 15)	22	(87)	0.1
Net earnings after taxes	$ 43,173	$ 11,400	SKr 197.3

Per share	*1973*	*1972*
Earnings before extraordinary items	$7.22	$1.70
Extraordinary items	0.22	0.27
Net earnings	$7.44	$1.97

Appropriations (see introduction to the notes)			
Reversal of undistributed earnings as above (note 9)	$ (2,845)	$ (875)	SKr (13.0)
Accumulated additional depreciation on property, plant and equipment sold (note 6)	1,510	1,072	6.9
Change in additional depreciation reserve (note 3)	(21,663)	3,326	(99.0)
Change in inventory reserve (note 8)	(24,726)	6,127	(113.0)
Deferred taxes (note 5)	23,742	(5,164)	108.5
Minority interest in appropriations (note 15)	2,078	(525)	9.5
Profit after appropriations	$ 21,269	$ 15,361	SKr 97.2

The United States Dollar amounts shown in the above statement represent translations from Swedish Kronor at the parity exchange rate at December 31, 1973 of SKr 4.57 to $1.00.

EXHIBIT 3.3C *Gränges AB NOTES*

Note 1—Sales to external customers

Breakdown of Total Sales by Companies	*1973*	*1972*
Gränges Aluminum	$ 107,000	$ 81,000
Gränges Mines	46,400	43,500
Gränges Hedlund	37,000	34,800
Gränges Metallverken	228,200	156,200
Gränges Nyby	122,800	75,300
Gränges Oxelösunds Järnverk	166,700	135,700
Gränges Shipping	62,400	57,300
Gränges TGOJ	27,800	25,000
Gränges Weda	60,800	50,300
Scanglas	25,600	23,600
Other business	57,300	49,700
Total sales	942,000	732,400
Sales between companies	68,300	56,900
External sales	$ 873,700	$ 675,500

Breakdown by Markets		
Sweden	$ 401,700	$ 332,800
EEC (incl. United Kingdom $45m., last year $21m.)	230,900	164,800
Rest of Western Europe	89,900	68,700
North, Central and South America	37,600	26,900
Others	53,600	26,900
	813,700	620,100
Gränges Shipping	60,000	55,400
External sales	$ 873,700	$ 675,500

Note 4—Breakdown by companies of operating profit after depreciation

	1973	*1972*
Gränges Aluminum	$ 9,300	$ (2,700)
Gränges Mines	0	3,800
Gränges Hedlund	1,400	1,300
Gränges Metallverken	24,100	8,000
Gränges Nyby	7,900	(3,200)

EXHIBIT 3.3C (continued) *Gränges AB NOTES*

Note 4—(cont.)

	1973	*1972*
Gränges Oxelösunds Järnverk	19,500	4,300
Gränges Shipping	10,700	3,100
Gränges TGOJ	3,500	1,100
Gränges Weda	2,800	1,600
Scanglas	4,700	3,500
Other business	2,500	(2,300)
Undistributed costs including Head Office	(4,700)	(3,600)
	$ 81,700	$ 14,900

Note 19—Stockholders' equity and capital employed

	1973	*1972*
Inventory reserve (note 8)	$ 100,328	$ 62,035
Investment fund	66	66
Accumulated additional depreciation, mainly untaxed (note 10)	230,809	213,960
(Additional depreciation includes depreciation on ships on order, $16.8m.)		
Untaxed reserves according to Balance Sheet	331,203	276,061
Less: Deferred taxes, 54% (54%) on untaxed reserves	169,800	140,000
Total reserves after deduction of deferred taxes	161,403	136,061
Less: Minority interests in the above reserves	8,580	6,255
Reserves referable to equity	152,823	129,806
Capital and reserves according to Balance Sheet	325,777	319,694
Stockholders' equity	478,600	449,500
Total assets according to Balance Sheet	$1,148,730	$1,054,420
Less: Operating liabilities	177,615	144,136
Capital employed	971,115	910,284

EXHIBIT 3.3C (continued) *Gränges AB NOTES*

Note 19—(cont.)

	1973	*1972*
Financed by		
Current loans and long-term liabilities according to Balance Sheet	303,041	303,085
Deferred taxes as above	169,800	140,000
	472,841	443,085
Minority interests in subsidiaries' equity	19,674	17,699
Total loans, etc.	492,515	460,784
Stockholders' equity as above	478,600	449,500
	$ 971,115	$ 910,284

Note 20—Breakdown by companies of capital employed (total assets according to Balance Sheet less operating liabilities)

	1973	*1972*
Gränges Aluminum	$ 104,800	$ 105,000
Gränges Mines	35,000	40,300
Gränges Hedlund	12,700	8,500
Gränges Metallverken	120,600	80,100
Gränges Nyby	109,200	100,400
Gränges Oxelösunds Järnverk	185,600	181,000
Gränges Shipping	70,700	77,700
Gränges TGOJ	35,000	37,200
Gränges Weda	35,000	36,500
Scanglas	26,900	24,500
Other business	42,200	38,100
Financial assets, etc.	193,400	181,000
	$ 971,100	$ 910,300

Note 21—Specification of internal sources of funds

	1973	*1972*
Net earnings after taxes	$ 43,173	$ 11,400
Items not influencing liquidity		
Depreciation charged to operating profit	47,505	43,676
Write-down of shares	1,511	—

EXHIBIT 3.3C (continued) *Gränges AB NOTES*

Note 21—(cont.)	*1973*	*1972*
Share in undistributed earnings of companies less than 50% owned	(2,845)	(875)
Deferred income taxes and adjustments	23,742	(5,164)
Capital gains on facilities sold, etc.	(3,829)	(284)
Price increase (decrease) on inventories (note 8)	13,567	(1,444)
Minority interests not added (deducted) above	2,078	(525)
Dividends	(15,230)	(15,230)
Total internal sources of funds	$ 109,672	$ 31,554

SOURCE: *The Accounting Review*, Vol. 46, Supplement 1976, pp. 96–98.

and a capital lease, even though the substance and intent of the two kinds of leases are different. Therefore, it is often the case abroad that a lease is a lease is a lease, simply because the term "lease" is used, even though in the United States various leases are treated differently because their substance is different.

Remaining Interpretation Problems

Even if all of the foregoing problems and difficulties were to be surmounted successfully, the analysis of foreign financial statements might still be misleading because the results of financial analysis are generally judged against *domestic* standards, that is, the standards of the analyzer's country, rather than against those of the country of the analyzed firm. In short, an inappropriate yardstick is being used to measure performance. A few examples will illustrate this situation.

In countries plagued by extensive inflation, it is considered good management to buy inventory as a hedge against inflation, to utilize debt financing extensively, and to maintain very low levels of monetary assets, that is limited liquidity. Applying standard U.S. financial analysis techniques to such a firm and judging the results against standard U.S. ratios would show the firm's debt-to-equity ratio as too high, its current and quick ratios as too low, and its inventory turnover as too slow. In short, the company would not appear to look well managed by American standards—a conclusion that may or may not be accurate, given the different and difficult environment in which that company operates.

A Japanese company typically shows enormous debt, slow collection of accounts and notes receivable, and very low profitability ratios. In short, it seems to be in bad shape by U.S. standards. But once again, appearances can be misleading. Among the members of a Japanese business group (called a *Keiretsu*), it is common to use interlocking debt to cement the business relationships among firms, and banks are typically members of each group, both as creditors and equity owners. Unlike the normal practice in the U.S., when a Japanese firm gets into financial trouble, its credit lines are extended rather than foreclosed. Finally, the extensive use in Japan of reserves and tax credits to minimize taxation also minimizes reported income because there is no distinction between tax and financial accounting. (In Japan and several other countries, if you do something for tax purposes, you must do it for financial reporting purposes—a situation different from that in the United States where one can use accelerated depreciation for tax purposes, lowering taxable income, but use straight-line depreciation for financial reporting purposes, increasing reported income.) When Japanese environmental factors are applied to the financial analysis of a Japanese firm, much of the short-term debt turns out to be long-term debt, and much of the long-term debt is really more a form of equity. Thus, the firm is not as deficient in liquid assets as it seems, and its reported profitability is lower than would have been reported using U.S. GAAP. A "standard" U.S. financial analysis would only generate misleading conclusions, then.

Unfortunately, there is no easy way to know whether the results of the financial analysis of foreign financial statements are misleading or accurate. One can be sure, though, that caution must be exercised. The more the analyzer knows about the cultural, legal, political, and economic environment of the firm's country, the more meaningful the financial analysis can be. International banks and accounting firms can often provide a great deal of such useful background information to an individual doing a financial analysis of a foreign firm.

Some Special Problems of Valuation and Income Determination for MNEs

So far, we have described some of the general differences in valuation and income determination in various countries and the problems these variations cause in conducting financial analysis. MNEs face the same problems because by definition they operate in different countries and hence use different accounting systems. For example, if an MNE consolidates it global operations for financial or tax-reporting purposes, it must put each of its foreign subsidiaries' financial statements into a common format, devise a univocal terminology, and possibly apply uniform accounting principles across the board. These consolidation problems will be discussed in greater detail in Chapter 5.

For proper management decision making, the MNE must have an *internal* accounting information system, too. Like the external reporting system, the internal system also must have a common format and a univocal language. These issues and problems will be discussed in Chapter 6.

Yet even if all countries were to use similar valuation and income determination procedures, the MNE would still have one major problem—which currency to use for its own valuation and income determination. For example, suppose an American firm's French subsidiary's inventory was worth $10,000 on February 1, when the French franc equalled $.25, and suppose the inventory remained unchanged until February 28, by which time the franc's value had dropped to $.20. If the French franc value of the inventory is considered to have remained at ff40,000, its translated U.S. dollar value has thereby fallen to $8,000. What is the best measure, then, of the inventory's value?

Or suppose a German subsidiary declares a 200,000 deutschmark dividend to its U.S. parent on April 1, but when it actually pays the dividend on May 1, the deutschmark has risen 10% in value against the dollar. Is the value of the dividend, and hence the income to the U.S. parent, 10% higher as a result of the change in the value of the deutschmark?

Suppose a company builds a $20 million plant in Brazil when the exchange rate was 10 pesos to the dollar; two years later, the exchange rate is 40 pesos to the dollar. Is the proper value of the plant $20 million, 800 million pesos,[4] or $5 million[5]? As we will show in Chapter 5, in the U.S. GAAP there are rules and procedures for the U.S. MNEs that face such situations, but many countries' accounting rules do not establish any guidelines for MNEs to follow.

Finally, a major problem for any MNE involves its accounting for

---

[4]$20,000,000 × 40 pesos per dollar = 800,000,000 pesos.

[5]$$\frac{\$20,000,000 \times 10 \text{ pesos per dollar}}{40 \text{ pesos per dollar}} = \$5,000,000.$$

inflation. Not only are inflation rates significantly different among countries, but the acceptable methods of accounting for inflation in each country also vary. The impact of inflation on proper valuation, income determination, and financial analysis is so important that we will devote the following chapter to a discussion of inflation accounting.

STUDY QUESTIONS FOR CHAPTER 3

1. Discuss the general relationship of valuation to income determination. What makes this relationship more complex for an MNE?
2. In other countries, what are some of the different valuation principles of fixed assets?
3. Why would certain countries allow the excessive depreciation of fixed assets?
4. Contrast the use of reserves in the United States with their use in other countries. What factors might explain different usage patterns?
5. From a company's standpoint, what are the advantages of income smoothing? From a financial analyst's perspective, what are the disadvantages of income smoothing?
6. From a company's standpoint, what are the advantages of "off-balance sheet" accounting? From a financial analyst's perspective, what problems are posed by off-balance sheet accounting?
7. What are the general shortcomings of ratio analyses? How are ratio analyses' shortcomings even more significant for analyzing foreign financial statements?
8. What are some of the other problems in analyzing foreign financial statements, and which one is the most difficult?
9. What are some of the peculiar problems of valuation and income determination for an MNE?

ADDITIONAL REFERENCES

1. American Accounting Association. "Report of the American Accounting Association Committee on International Accounting, 1974–75." *Accounting Review*, Supplement 1976, pp. 70–196.
2. American Institute of Certified Public Accountants. *Professional Accounting in 30 Countries.* New York: AICPA, 1975.

3. Bedford, Norton M., and Gautier, Jacques P. "An International Analytical Comparison of the Structure and Content of Annual Reports in the European Economic Community, Switzerland and the United States." *International Journal of Accounting*, Spring 1974, pp. 1–44.

4. Choi, Frederick D. S., and Muller, Gerhard G. *An Introduction to Multinational Accounting*. Englewood Cliffs, N.J.: Prentice-Hall, 1978, Chapter 2.

5. Clapp, Charles L. "National Variations in Accounting Principles and Practices." *International Journal of Accounting*, Fall 1967, pp. 29–42.

6. Davidson, Sidney, and Kohlmeier, John M. "A Measure of the Impact of Some Foreign Accounting Principles." *International Journal of Accounting*, Fall 1967, pp. 183–212.

7. Gray, S. J. *EEC Accounting and Reporting: A Comparative Guide to Legal Requirements*. International Centre for Research in Accounting, 1976.

8. Hatfield, H. R. "Some Variations in Accounting Practice in England, France, Germany and the United States." *Journal of Accounting Research*, Autumn 1966, pp. 169–182.

9. Institute of Chartered Accountants in England and Wales (ICAEW). *Accounting Principles and Practices in European Countries*. 1972.

10. Lafferty, Michael. *Accounting in Europe*. Cambridge, England: Woodhead, Faulkner, 1976. Published in association with National Westminster Bank.

11. Mueller, Gerhard. "Accounting Principles Generally Accepted in the United States versus Those Generally Accepted Elsewhere." *International Journal of Accounting*, Spring 1968, pp. 91ff.

12. Oldham, K. M. *Accounting Systems and Practice in Europe*. Farnsborough, Hampshire, England: Gower, 1975.

Chapter 4

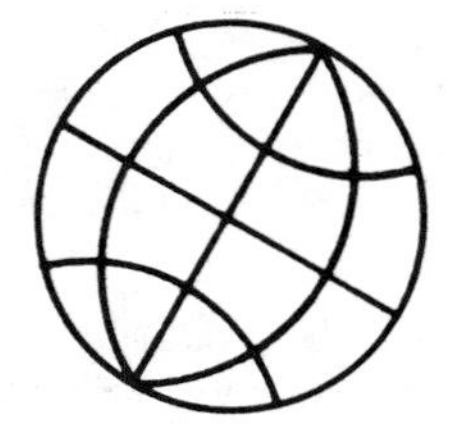

Inflation Accounting

WORLDWIDE INFLATION AND FINANCIAL REPORTING

Inflation is not new, nor does it appear to trouble the economic life of only a few countries. In fact, inflation is so common and persistent throughout the world that the relevant question is not *whether* there will be inflation, but only *how much* inflation there will be. While almost all countries have experienced some inflation, several countries have had truly staggering levels. Argentina, for example, found itself struggling with inflation rates of 182.3% in 1975, 443.2% in 1976, 176.1% in 1977, and 175.5% in 1978. Other examples of inflation rates for various nations and regions, based on the consumer price index for 1974 through 1981, are presented in Exhibit 4.1.

Inflation not only affects the real purchasing power of money; it also affects the quality and usefulness of financial reports. Thus, the problem of accounting in an inflationary economic environment has been continuously discussed. When prices are stable, the traditional approach of historical cost accounting probably provides both an objective indicator of value and a basis for judging the performance and efficiency of mangement. Financial statements based on historical cost accounting in economically stable times enable those doing a financial analysis to compare the results of one period with another. However,

EXHIBIT 4.1 Consumer Price Index for Selected Years (1975 = 100)

	1974	*1975*	*1976*	*1977*	*1978*	*1979*	*1980*	*1981*
World	15.3%	13.6%	11.1%	11.4%	9.8%	12.2%	15.5%	14.1%
Industrial Countries	13.1	10.8	8.3	8.4	7.2	9.2	11.9	10.0
Developing Countries—Oil Exporting	16.3	18.0	15.9	15.2	10.6	10.4	14.0	13.0
Developing Countries—Non-Oil Exporting	28.3	28.6	26.0	27.9	24.9	30.2	37.5	34.8
Europe	18.3	17.9	15.1	19.7	25.1	33.2	50.2	32.0
Western Hemisphere	30.4	44.9	55.3	48.3	41.5	47.6	56.1	63.0
Argentina	—	182.3	443.2	176.1	175.5	159.5	100.8	104.5
Brazil	27.6	28.9	42.0	43.7	38.7	52.7	82.8	105.5
Chile	505.5	374.6	211.8	91.9	40.1	33.4	35.1	20.4
France	13.7	11.7	9.6	9.4	9.1	10.7	13.3	13.3
Germany	7.0	5.9	4.3	3.6	2.8	4.1	5.5	5.9
Ghana	24.2	41.2	52.7	116.4	73.1	54.4	50.1	117.0
Italy	19.1	17.0	16.8	17.0	12.1	14.7	21.2	17.8
Japan	24.3	11.9	9.3	8.1	3.8	3.6	8.0	4.9
Mexico	22.5	16.8	15.9	29.1	17.3	18.2	26.4	27.9
Netherlands	9.6	10.5	8.8	6.4	4.1	4.2	6.5	6.7
New Zealand	11.2	14.5	16.9	14.5	11.9	13.8	17.1	15.3
Peru	16.9	23.6	33.5	38.1	57.8	66.7	59.2	75.4
Turkey	15.9	19.2	17.3	27.1	45.3	58.7	110.2	36.6
United Kingdom	16.0	24.2	16.5	15.9	8.3	13.4	18.0	11.9
United States	10.9	9.2	5.8	6.5	7.5	11.3	13.5	10.4
Uruguay	77.2	81.4	50.6	58.2	44.5	66.8	63.5	34.1
Zaire	27.5	30.7	85.1	63.1	58.4	97.7	36.8	30.0

SOURCE: *International Financial Statistics*, published by the International Monetary Fund.

when prices are changing, as in an inflationary period, the usefulness and relevance of information provided by the historical cost approach become doubtful.

It also has been argued that in an inflationary period financial statements based on historical cost accounting that are prepared in different countries cannot necessarily be considered comparable. Since the rate of inflation may differ from country to country, the effects on the quality and the usefulness of financial statements may vary. Still, it is not clear what approach to accounting for inflation would make the financial statements of different nations more comparable.

Overview of the Accounting Response to Inflation

Over the last few decades countries have made many attempts to deal with the effects of inflation on accounting reports. However, whenever inflation somewhat subsides, these countries typically revert to the historical cost standard, which has been prevalent throughout the entire existence of financial accounting.

Suggestions of a *continuous* accounting response to the impact of inflation on a country were first made in the period after World War I in central Europe, particularly in Germany. This movement was led, among others by Schmidt, Limperg, and Schmalenbach.[1] Schmidt and Limperg suggested that an enterprise must retain its true economic value by annually revaluing its assets to reflect their market value. Schmalenbach, on the other hand, believed that a general price index might be more practical than the individual valuation of assets. Yet, though discussed in theory in various European Countries, these approaches were never put into practice. They were deemed unsuitable largely because after currency adjustments took place a new basis for financial accounting was found. That is, all financial statements were recast in the new post-war currency. A significant decline in the inflationary rate followed this recasting and, as a result, the accounting profession was reluctant to put theoretical proposals for inflation accounting into practice.

It had become apparent, however, that inflation was a major prob-

[1]F. Schmidt, *Die Organische Bilanz im Rahmen der Wirtschaft*, Leipzig, 1921; T. Limperg, Jr., *Enige Beschouwingen over Kostprijs en Prijsvorming als Bedrijfshuishoudkundig Probleem* (Bedrijfs Econ. Studien, 1932); and Eugene Schmalenbach, *Dynamische Bilanz*, (Leipzig, 1919).

lem, and that there were two possible responses to the inflation-related accounting issues, namely:

1. Accountants could adjust all financial statements at one point in time and continue on the "new historical basis."
2. Accountants could design a procedure which would continuously provide adjustments.

After World War II, inflation once again surfaced, and new responses were advanced by the accounting profession. In most European countries a one-time adjustment (to be discussed later) was chosen to put financial statements in order. France was the only European country that used an indexing approach and it did so until 1950. In South American countries, inflation could not be brought under control and, therefore, several countries reverted to an indexing method. The Netherlands permitted a replacement valuation as an equally valid option to historical valuation.

During the decades following the 1960s inflation once again became a serious worldwide problem. New approaches to inflation accounting have been adopted, or are presently under study, to deal with the severity of inflation in various countries. Although the United States had experienced various levels of inflation, it was not until the 1970s period of persistent double-digit inflation that the U.S. took major action with regard to inflation accounting.

Proposed Approaches to Inflation Accounting

Accounting scholars have proposed, examined, and experimented with various ways of accounting for the effects of inflation. A clearly acceptable solution to this problem, however, has yet to emerge, because the accounting profession both cannot reach a consensus on the objectives of financial reporting, and has yet to develop a complete conceptual framework for accounting. It is the premise here that the objectives of financial reporting should be the major factors in selecting both a proper asset-valuation concept and an acceptable approach to determining income. In other words, the premise is that objectives determine valuation standards, each of which satisfies a specific purpose, need, or use. Any debate over the use of one valuation standard versus another is meaningless in this context without relating the valuation standard to the need for fulfilling a specific objective.

Four basic models related to asset valuation and income determination have been discussed in the accounting literature: (1) Historical Cost Accounting (HCA); (2) Price Level Adjusted Historical Cost Accounting (PLA/HC); (3) Current Value Accounting (CVA); and (4) Price Level Adjusted/Current Value Accounting (PLA/CV). The following example illustrates how these models are applied in inflation accounting.

Assume that a parcel of land is purchased on January 1, 1982 for $10,000. The Gross National Product Implicit Price Deflator increases 20% during 1982, and the quoted market price of the land on December 31, 1982 is $15,000. The value of the land and of the *holding gain* as of December 31, 1982, under each of these models for inflation accounting are as follows:

	HCA	*PLA/HC*	*CVA*	*PLA/CV*
Land, 1/1/1982	$10,000	$10,000	$10,000	$10,000
Restatement to reflect inflation (20%)	—	12,000	—	12,000
Land, 12/31/1982	10,000	12,000	15,000	15,000
Holding gain	$ 0	$ 0	$ 5,000	$ 3,000

The reported net income on 12/31/1982 under each of these models is as follows:

Income from operations (assumed)	$ 0	$ 0	$ 0	$ 0
Holding gain	0	0	5,000	3,000
Reported net income	$ 0	$ 0	$ 5,000	$ 3,000

Examining these results, one could argue that historical cost accounting is irrelevant in an inflationary economic environment, since it does not disclose the effect of inflation on an enterprise's financial position or on the results of its operations. The second model, price level adjusted historical cost accounting, fails to account for the effect of inflation on nonmonetary items and, as such, deals only with gains and losses in purchasing power. PLA/HC also fails to report the current value of net assets as of the balance sheet date and therefore does not report the true financial position of the firm.

Current value accounting does consider changes in nonmonetary items, but then ignores the gains and losses on holding net monetary items. It is argued that when the purchasing prices of nonmonetary assets change, using replacement costs to make charges against the revenues of the period will serve to maintain the operating capacity of the firm. However, it is doubtful that a firm would be able to replace its physical capacity with the accumulated amounts for replacement. On the date of replacement, the purchase price may far exceed the accumulated amounts for that purpose (because actual prices have probably exceeded the conservative estimates used for depreciation).

The final approach, price level adjusted/current value accounting, of course represents the combination of current value accounting and price level accounting. The use of current value purchasing power units (CVPuPU) would characterize this approach.

Note that whatever the approach proposed for inflation accounting is, it is imperative that the purchasing power of the capital invested in a business always be maintained. In addition, an income statement should disclose the effect of inflation on *all* balance sheet items, and not just the effect of inflation on net monetary items. CVPuPU, an approach similar to that proposed by Sterling and Chambers,[2] satisfies these two requirements, and emphasizes that price level accounting and current value accounting are in fact complementary approaches to solving the problems associated with accounting in an inflationary environment. The point here is that while price level accounting deals with the overall changes in the purchasing power of money, current value accounting deals with the changes in the relative values of specific assets (that is, with specific price changes).

Under the CVPuPU approach, assets are valued at their current sales value as of the balance sheet date (in contrast to replacement cost accounting which reports assets based on their purchase prices). In addition, the income statement would report all realized and unrealized gains and losses from holding monetary and nonmonetary net assets. This type of presentation would ultimately help the users of financial statements obtain a fair idea of the financial position of a firm as of a specific date, and to see the results of operations for an accounting period.

If only one universal set of financial statements for external reporting purposes seems to be the practical solution to the inflation accounting dilemma, then CVPuPU finds itself both well grounded in theory and easily applied in practice. One limitation of PLA/CV, however, can be identified. It lies in the possibility that a ready market for many of the

---

[2]Robert R. Sterling, "Relevant Financial Reporting in an Age of Price Changes," *Journal of Accountancy* (February 1975); and Raymond J. Chambers, "NOD, COG and PuPU: See How Inflation Teases!," *Journal of Accountancy* (September 1975).

assets of a firm may not exist. Thus, market values for these assets may be impossible to compute. However, this shortcoming is not insurmountable: it can be overcome by utilizing the next best available prices for these assets (for example, replacement or liquidation values).

Despite its ability to account for the effects of inflation, the CVPuPU or PLA/CV approach is not without its detractors. There are those in the accounting profession who claim that it mixes apples and oranges and so cannot be depended upon as an appropriate approach for asset valuation. Still, their point is open to challenge, since changes in both specific and general prices occur concurrently in an inflationary period. Keeping this in mind, the income statement should disclose all of these changes, and should attempt to maintain the integrity of the invested capital in the calculation of the profit for each accounting period.

APPLICATION OF INFLATION ACCOUNTING IN SELECTED COUNTRIES

As noted earlier, the responses to inflation, as far as accounting is concerned, have varied throughout the world according to the severity of the inflation. Countries either have adopted a one-time adjustment or make continuous adjustments of financial statements to make them more relevant to the environment in which they are prepared. A review of the accounting for inflation in several different countries follows.

Germany

Germany experienced two serious inflationary periods in its recent history, after World War I and World War II. During these years of inflation, the usefulness and relevance of financial data based on historical cost accounting were questionable. German scholars suggested various proposals to account for the effect of inflation on accounting reports, such as Schmalenbach's current purchasing power method, proposed in 1919, and Schmidt's current value accounting, proposed in 1921. The 1924 currency reform in Germany brought with it a law called the *Goldmarkbilanzgesetz*, the features of which were very similar to those of a later law, the *DM Eröffnungsbilanzgesetz*, a law passed on August 29, 1948, which concerned (deutsche mark) opening financial statements. These laws required all businesses to restate accounting data for financial statements and tax purposes. The last supplementary law pertaining to the revaluation of balance sheets, finally passed on June 6, 1955, regulated the revaluation of securities.

From a valuation point of view, all German companies had a fresh start in 1948. Balance sheet continuity was affected only in that the law required all balance sheet items appearing on preceding balance sheets to be shown on a new balance sheet. Section 5 of the law contains the general valuation standard, by prescribing that "assets cannot be stated at an amount exceeding their value on the date of the balance sheet." This valuation standard reflects the underlying purpose of the law, which was to restate all assets at amounts approximating current replacement cost as nearly as possible. Although the valuation requirements of the new law gave companies substantial freedom within the given limits, it can still be said that the resulting financial statements were at last realistic and offered a fair basis for intercompany comparisons. Most companies used fairly realistic current values since they preferred the more tangible and immediate benefits of tax-deductible depreciation to any savings in the war-damage levies, which were payable in installments over a 25-year period.

The German balance sheet law of 1948 represented an attempt to achieve uniform balance sheet values at current prices. Although the final results were not ideal, the main purpose of establishing a new and sound basis for financial reporting and taxation purposes was certainly attained. The balance sheets for the periods following the DM opening balance sheet were again subject to the rules of the German company act and the German commercial code, which meant that the historical cost standard and the standard of the lower-of-cost-or-market were fully applicable again. In the years since the initial currency reform, the financial statements have become somewhat distorted again because price levels in Germany, as in the United States, have risen gradually and consistently.

France

France's experience with inflation mirrored the German case. After World War II, inflation was particularly rampant. The French wholesale price index (1948 = 100) rose from 16.19 in 1944 to 192.50 in 1958. Although France permitted some revaluation of fixed assets after 1928, few businesses made use of this provision. So, during the period from 1945–1959 France passed several laws and decrees which made revaluation mandatory. The replacement cost of a fixed asset was derived from multiplying its acquisition cost by the quotient of the official index of the current year divided by the official index of the acquisition year.

The rapid inflation in France in the years following the Second World War made a departure from the historical cost standard necessary. Balance sheet valuations at current values were allowed, but specific directives on the methods to be employed were outlined in a number of decrees. With the introduction of the new franc (*nouveau franc*) in 1959, the revaluation of assets was discontinued after one final restatement. The historical cost standard was made mandatory again, and valuation rules again were quite similar to those practiced in America. According to the provisions of the 1959 new franc law, businesses with sales in excess of ff 500,000,000 were required to make one final revaluation of assets by December 31, 1962.

In dealing with inflation, the French developed methods of revaluing assets that attempted to eliminate price-level effects from financial statements. The primary method was to use price-level coefficients based on the wholesale price indices of those commodities which largely determined the cost of most fixed assets. The French method, therefore, attempted to eliminate only the inflationary price-level effects of the selected commodities reflected in the revaluation coefficients. Price changes caused by shifts in demand, or changes in technology, were eliminated only when reflected in the combined index.

More recently, the French government attempted to deal with the fact that the revaluation coefficients generally ignored the inflation resulting from those shifts in demand or changes in technology by issuing the Finance Acts of 1977 and 1978. These laws mandated the use of current value accounting for the companies listed whose fiscal years ended after December 1977. The Finance Acts also called for the primary financial statements of the listed companies to report all assets on a current replacement cost basis. However, this replacement cost could not exceed the net book value multiplied by an official coefficient. A revaluation account would then be established for the adjustment of all assets, and this account would be reported within the stockholders' equity section of the balance sheet.

Chile

To compensate for inflation, Chilean enterprises are permitted to revalue some of their fixed assets in accordance with two laws. The first law was passed in 1954 and requires revaluation as approved by the superintendency of corporations. Companies are asked to set up a revaluation of fixed assets account on the owners' equity side of the balance sheet to record such revaluations. The second law, passed in 1964, permits companies to revalue their invested capital on the basis of the variations occurring in the cost-of-living index. The index of the months immediately preceding the financial statement's date is used and compared with the index of the same months in the previous year. Index data are supplied by the National Statistical Services for this computation. Invested capital is regarded as the difference between assets and liabilities, excluding intangibles and certain deferred assets. The difference computed for revaluation is exempt from all taxes and is considered to be invested capital.

Since the revaluations are based on invested capital, these amounts have to be distributed on the asset side. They are to be allocated in the following manner:

1. Tangible assets will receive the same percentage by which the invested capital has been revalued.
2. The allocation basis is the book value.
3. No revaluation can be applied to unpaid amounts for fixed assets which are purchased with foreign currency. In this particular case, both the asset and the liability accounts are adjusted in accordance with the exchange rate existing at the balance sheet date.

Investments are revalued in accordance with the prequoted stock exchange price on the financial statement's date. If no quotations are available, the acquisition costs are adjusted by the same percentage by which the invested capital has been revalued. The remainder of the revaluation amount is charged to the profit and loss statement; however, this amount is limited to 20% of the taxable income for the year (before the charge is made).

It should be noted that revaluation is based on a residual amount, and that certain items can be charged to the profit and loss statement tax free. Also note that revaluations of investments to their quoted market value must go through a "reserve for the fluctuation of investments" account, which constitutes a nondistributable reserve on the credit side of the balance sheet.

The Netherlands

Accounting and business economics are closely related in the Netherlands. Therefore, economic concepts of income, cost, and value have had a great impact on accounting concepts. This alliance explains the wide acceptance of sound business-economic standards as the guiding force in the development of Dutch accounting standards. The 1970 Act on Annual Accounts states that accounting practices should "comply with standards that are regarded as being acceptable in economic and social life."[3] Thus, the use of replacement value accounting in the Netherlands stems from the firmly held belief that accounting must first of all make sense from a business-economics viewpoint. Profit is therefore measured as the maximum that could be spent while still leaving the entity as "well off" at the end of the period as it was at the beginning.

The Dutch laws on financial statements do not contain detailed regulation of the standards for profit determination. It only requires that companies use valuation methods which are acceptable in business practice. If historical cost accounting does not present fairly the value of investments or physical assets, then additional information on current values and related current costs should be included in the financial statements.

Although the majority of companies quoted on the national stock exchange still use the historical cost standard, most *major* companies on the stock exchange use current value accounting. As discussed by Limperg fifty years ago, current replacement value accounting is based on the assumption that a company is going to continue its operations long into the future. To remain profitable, the actual value of goods and services available for sale must be smaller than their sales value. This is necessary because the company must replace those goods and services. When the input prices in the market (for example, the prices of labor, equipment, and material) have gone up or have been subject to some change, the comparison of the replacement value with the sales value clearly becomes the only acceptable measure of profit.

Analysis of business practices in the Netherlands shows that companies use the replacement valuation largely to restate and properly value physical assets on the balance sheet and to adjust profits for inflation. Revalued items tend to be land, buildings, machinery, and inventories, with replacement values usually based on index numbers, appraisals for insurance purposes, company estimates, and/or information from suppliers.

When companies do not plan to replace the assets, the net realizable value is more often used than the replacement value. In some instances,

[3]Act on Annual Accounts of Enterprises (*Wet op de Jaarrekening Van Ondernemingen*), 1970, Article 5.

however, companies incorporate technological changes into their estimates of replacement value which ultimately lead to new deviations from external data. Although a lower percentage of revaluation is often used for some of these, in about one-third of the cases of revaluation either individual estimates or estimates by means of cost comparisons with other companies are used.[4]

In all cases of revaluation where replacement valuation is used, companies determine depreciation on the basis of the new higher value. Backlog depreciation is rarely taken into consideration, a fact which seems to provide support for the argument that replacement valuation is insufficient to fully maintain the capital substance of a company. It would seem, then, that the theory of replacement valuation as stated by Limperg has not completely adopted into actual business practice in the Netherlands. Few companies appear to be concerned with the theoretical exactness of their computations. Since most Dutch companies rely heavily on internal financing, they are interested in preventing the distribution of too many dividends which ultimately would result in the erosion of that internal financing.[5]

The Netherlands Institute of Registered Accountants (NIVRA) has lent strong support to the application of replacement value accounting in Holland. According to Henk Volten, General Director of NIVRA, the present position of the Institute includes the following:

- A clear preference for current value application as the basis for financial reporting.
- Acceptance of a minimal position, whereby financial statements are based upon historical cost, under the expressed condition that in such a case the notes must contain additional information concerning profit and equity on the basis of current values.[6]

These preferences indicate NIVRA's flexible attitude that allows companies to utilize the best means they have when applying the replacement value concept.

[4]When revaluation occurs, it is most frequently undertaken on an annual basis; however, there are some companies which undertake revaluation after longer periods of time, such as two, three, or even four years.

[5]For more information on replacement value theory in the Netherlands, see "Report of the Committee on International Accounting," *Accounting Review*, Supplement 1976, pp. 107–133.

[6]Henk Voltin, "A Response from the Netherlands," *Journal of Accountancy* (March 1978).

One of the best known firms using replacement valuation is the Philips Company in Eindhoven, Netherlands. A description and explanation of Philips's inflation accounting procedure, along with a copy of a statement of its valuation standards, can be found in the appendix to this chapter (pp. 114–18).

Brazil

Brazil has experienced so much inflation that historical cost accounting is completely invalid there. Hence, the Brazilian government in 1964 introduced inflation accounting into the tax laws, and adopted a system of monetary correction called "indexing." Indexing was viewed also as a means of stimulating foreign investments in Brazil. Some success in this was achieved, according to most indications, and the high inflation rate was reduced partly because of the indexing approach.

Brazilian accounting is regulated by Corporation Law No. 6404 of December 15, 1976, which establishes all of the accounting and reporting requirements for all individual corporations and groups of companies. This law requires owners' equity accounts and "permanent assets" to be adjusted at the end of each accounting period using a price index compiled by the government, the readjustable government treasury bond index. "Permanent assets" are defined as property, plant, equipment, deferred charges, and related amortizations. The adjustment procedure is basically the application of a general price level (constant peso) index to revalue certain, but not all, balance sheet accounts.

The difference between the adjusted owners' equity accounts and the "permanent assets" is called the net monetary correction. If the equity position is *greater* than the permanent asset position, the monetary correction is charged to income for book and tax purposes. If the owners' equity position is *less* than the permanent asset position, the monetary correction is *not* charged to income, but is assigned to a capital account entitled "reserve for unrealized profit." Some long-term liabilities are also adjusted for changes in purchasing power, and are charged to income. However, such adjustments are considered part of operating income, and are separate from the monetary correction. Finally, some corporations are encouraged, based on market values, to revalue some of their other assets at the end of each accounting period and to estabish a contra account under stockholders' equity called "revaluation reserves." Depreciation, in this case, is based on the new value.

United Kingdom

The rapid escalation of prices in the United Kingdom in the late 1960s and 1970s had such a tremendous effect on the operations of companies that the accounting profession was forced to reexamine its generally accepted accounting standards. In response to inflationary pressures, the Institute of Chartered Accountants in England and Wales issued the Provisional Statement of Standard Accounting Practice No. 7 in May, 1974, entitled "Accounting for Changes in the Purchasing Power of Money," which recommended that companies prepare price-level adjusted financial statements on a supplementary basis. It closely resembled the recommendation made by the American Institute of Certified Public Accountants in APB Satement No. 3, "Financial Statements Restated for General Price-Level Changes," with the exception of the price index to be used. In the British standard the use of the Retail Price Index (RPI) was recommended, whereas the AICPA upheld the Gross National Product Implicit Price Deflator (GNP Deflator) as the best indicator of changes in the general purchasing power of money.

Because there was some disagreement on the proper approach to inflation accounting in the United Kingdom, an Inflation Accounting Committee was appointed by the British government. The Committee submitted its report and recommendations in September, 1975, which became known as the Sandilands report. The Sandilands report rejected price-level accounting in favor of current value accounting as the only long-term solution to inflation accounting. Historic cost statements were to be eliminated entirely, and revaluations were to be based on a set of government published indices for 52 classes of capital assets and inventory.

Not to be outdone by a government-sponsored committee, the Accounting Standards Committee of the Institute of Chartered Accountants issued its own Exposure Draft (ED 18) which reversed its earlier stand on supplementary price-level adjusted statements by recommending a modification of the Sandilands report to include additional disclosure of gains and losses on monetary assets and liabilities. However, disagreement among the Institute's members led to a defeat of ED 18—primarily over the required elimination of historic cost accounting. After more deliberation, the Accounting Standards Committee developed still another approach in 1977, known as the Hyde Guidelines. These guidelines were subsequently transformed in 1979 into Exposure Draft 24, "Current Cost Accounting"—combining both constant dollar *and* current cost approaches, but on a supplementary basis. After more deliberation, ED 24 became the basis for the current United Kingdom standard, the "Statement of Standard Accounting Practice 16: Current Cost Accounting," (SSAP #16), issued in March of 1980.

SSAP #16 represents a three-year experiment in inflation accounting to be evaluated in 1983. It covers all publicly traded companies, nationalized firms, and other firms above a certain size, and requires them to disclose in their annual reports the following current cost information:[7]

1. A current cost profit and loss account with
   (a) the current cost operating profit derived after making depreciation, cost of sales, and "monetary working capital" adjustments, and
   (b) the current cost profit (after operations) attributable to shareholders derived after a "gearing adjustment" has been made.
2. A current cost balance sheet with
   (a) the fixed assets and inventory at net current replacement cost, and
   (b) a capital maintenance reserve to reflect revaluation surplus and deficits, the "monetary working capital" adjustment, and the "gearing" adjustment.
3. Current cost earnings per share.

The "gearing adjustment" shows the benefits to stockholders from inflation when business operations are financed by net borrowings. An adjustment is made to the difference between total liabilities and monetary assets excluding trade receivables and payables already adjusted in the "monetary working capital adjustment" (MWCA). The MWCA shows the inflationary impact on trade payables minus trade receivables, and is considered an adjustment to income. The gearing adjustment is included in the final profit figure for the firm.

Finally, SSAP #16 allows firms to present current cost information (1) as a supplement to historic cost accounts, (2) as the primary accounts, with historic cost accounts as supplements, or (3) as the only accounts (provided adequate historical cost information accompanies them).

---

[7]See "Statement of Standard Accounting Practice No. 16: Current Cost Accounting," *Accountancy*, April 1980, pp. 99–110.

United States

Accounting for inflation has been a topic debated in the U.S. for many decades. The first complete discussion of this topic was presented in the mid-1930s by Henry Sweeney in his *Stabilized Accounting.*[8] The problem of accounting in an inflationary economy, however, became more acute in the U.S. after World War II. The 1970s brought a noticeable increase in the inflation rate; and so more attention was paid to inflation accounting.

In December, 1974, the Financial Accounting Standards Board (FASB) released an Exposure Draft, *Financial Reporting in Units of General Purchasing Power,*[9] which required that a comprehensive restatement of financial statements be presented on a supplementary basis, using the GNP Implicit Price Deflator. However, the issuance of an official statement by FASB on this topic was deferred, apparently to await the outcome of the results of an experiment with the Securities and Exchange Commission's Accounting Series Release ASR No. 190, issued on March 23, 1976.

ASR No. 190, "Notice of Adoption of Amendments to Regulation S-X Requiring Disclosure of Certain Replacement Cost Data," required a footnote disclosure of replacement cost data for inventories, cost of goods sold, productive capacity, depreciation, depletion, and amortization in financial statements filed with the SEC for fiscal years ending on or after December 25, 1976.[10] The objective of this release was to provide information to investors which would help them make decisions about the strength of an enterprise. Replacement cost was defined as "the lowest amount that would have to be paid in the normal course of business to obtain an asset of equivalent operating or productive capacity."[11] This release applied to all registrants whose total inventories plus gross property, plant, and equipment, were more than $100 million and at the same time were more than 10% of total assets. About

---

[8]Henry W. Sweeney, *Stabilized Accounting* (New York: Harper Bros., 1936).

[9]Financial Accounting Standards Board, *Financial Reporting in Units of General Purchasing Power,* Exposure Draft (Stamford, Conn.: FASB, December 31, 1974).

[10]Securities and Exchange Commission, "Notice of Adoption of Amendments to Regulation S-X Requiring Disclosure of Certain Replacement Cost Data," Accounting Series Release No. 190 (Washington, D.C.: SEC, March 23, 1976).

[11]________________, "Notice of Publication of Staff Accounting Bulletin No. 7," Staff Accounting Bulletin No. 7 (Washington, D.C.: SEC, March 23, 1976).

1,000 of the nation's largest industrial corporations were thus qualified and had to comply with ASR No. 190.

This pronouncement represented the first official step taken in the U.S. toward implementing current value accounting. In short, it required replacement cost data to be disclosed on a supplementary basis for those financial statements filed with the SEC. However, ASR No. 190, not accounting for the effects of inflation on monetary items, met with criticism. It was also considered deficient for not requiring the disclosure of financial statements prepared solely on a replacement cost accounting basis. Finally, opponents of ASR No. 190 contended that the costs of its implemention were excessive. In one recent survey of twenty large corporations, for example, it was found that the cost of implementing ASR. No. 190 was somewhere between $5,000 and $800,000 per firm.[12]

Faced with these shortcomings, and with the pressure placed on the accounting profession to develop an official position on inflation accounting, FASB issued Statement No. 33 in September, 1979, entitled "Financial Reporting and Changing Prices."[13] The Consumer Price Index for all Urban Consumers (CPI-U), according to this statement, would be used for price-level data, and current cost data would be determined by direct pricing, indexation, or standard costing. Upon the issuance of FAS No. 33, the SEC rescinded ASR No. 190.

Based on FAS No. 33, companies whose total inventories and property, plant, and equipment (before deducting accumulated depreciation) are more than $125 million, or whose total assets (after deducting accumulated depreciation) are more than $1 billion are required to disclose, on a supplementary basis, the following information:

1. Income from continuing operations based on an historical cost price-level adjusted standard.
2. The purchasing power gain or loss on net monetary items.
3. Income from continuing operations on a current cost basis.
4. Current cost amounts of inventory and property, plant, and equipment at the end of the accounting period.

---

[12]C.W. Bastable, "Is SEC Replacement Cost Data Worth the Effort?," *Journal of Accountancy* (October 1977).

[13]Financial Accounting Standards Board, *Financial Reporting and Changing Prices*, Statement of Financial Accounting Standards No. 33 (Stamford, Conn.: FASB, September 1979).

5. Increases or decreases in current cost amounts of inventory and property, plant, and equipment, as a net of inflation.
6. A five-year summary of selected financial data, including information on income, sales, and other operating revenues, net assets, dividends per common share, and the market price per share. In addition, when computing net assets, only inventory and property, plant, and equipment need to be adjusted for the effects of changing prices.

FASB, therefore, has retained the historical cost standard as the basis for the preparation of primary financial statements and has required the disclosure of supplementary information related to both price-level and current cost accounting. Some leaders of the accounting profession have voiced strong feelings that it is not yet time for the United States to depart from historical cost accounting. For example, Robert T. Sprouse, the Vice-Chairman of FASB, stated:

> Financial accounting in the U.S. is likely to continue to be based primarily on historical costs and exchange transactions. A great deal remains to be learned about implementing the use of other measures that are likely to be confined to supplemental disclosures.[14]

SUMMARY AND CONCLUSION

Inflation calls for immediate action on the part of the accounting profession. Although it may be argued that profit increases and decreases are equalized in the long run, there is no evidence that inflation will ultimately subside or recede. The issue of the time-lag error that arises in all financial statements based on historical cost, therefore, demands attention.

The responses of the accounting profession to inflation have varied throughout the world in proportion to the severity of that inflation. As we argued earlier, since accounting is a product of the environment, it is influenced by environmental forces, social, cultural, legal, political, and economic. Thus, in an inflationary environment, it would seem wise for accountants to adopt standards which would help disclose the effects of the inflation on both the financial position and the result of operations of an enterprise. As we have seen, different approaches to

[14]Robert T. Sprouse, "News Features," *Journal of Accountancy* (October 1977).

inflation accounting have been applied throughout the world, the most important of them being replacement value accounting. We have suggested that if only one universal set of financial statements for external reporting purposes is going to be prepared in an inflationary economy, then the current value purchasing power units (CVPuPU) standard is preferable.

The necessity for a simplified approach may account for the adoption of price-level accounting based on a general price index in countries such as Chile and Brazil. Yet, it is doubtful that such an approach, utilizing a crude measure of valuation as it does, would be adopted for the valuation of assets in a developed country like the United Kingdom. The use of more precise standards for assets valuation seems more applicable to the accounting problems of the more developed nations.

APPENDIX[15]

To determine its financial position and the results of its operations, the Philips Company revalues assets using several different methods. All inventories are maintained at standard costs. Departments in charge of certain inventories rely on information provided by purchasing departments to prepare inventories for groups of similar material, taking into consideration all price trends. All price indices are closely watched, and as soon as they depart from the previous standard cost basis developed for the inventories, an adjustment is made. If the inventory account is debited, the credit goes to an account called "replacement value adjustment to stocks," which is part of the capital revaluation reserves. The individual inventory accounts are always maintained at the standard cost at the beginning of the period, and adjustments are usually made at the end of the year. Adjustments may be made more frequently than this, however.

The Philips Company also calculates losses on monetary assets by means of making reference to the cost-of-living index. All such adjustments are posted to an account called "reserve for diminishing purchasing power of nominal assets," and are charged against the revenues of the period. For this purpose, nominal assets are defined as monetary assets less liabilities.

---

[15]SOURCE: Adolph Enthoven, "The 1973 Annual Report of N.V. Philips—The Netherlands," *The Accounting Review*, Vol. 46, Supplement 1976, pp. 123–124.

Sales prices are accepted as representing the proper values for income statement purposes, and expenses, therefore, must be adjusted. The cost-of-goods-sold adjustment follows a procedure similar to the one described for inventories. Adjustments are made frequently, however, so that by the end of the period the total cost of goods sold represents an average of the period. As stated above, indices used for this evaluation are based on a group of related products. Revaluation of depreciation amounts are done only periodically and are computed by the company based on its own indices. When they are done after the fact, revaluations for depreciation are written off against the capital reserve account so that the profit will not be affected.

A similar procedure is used for all other expenses. If prices decline and reserve accounts are thereby exhausted, the amount of potential debits are charged against profits for the period.

APPENDIX CONTINUED: EXPLANATORY NOTES TO THE COMBINED STATEMENTS OF THE PHILIPS COMPANY

These statements combine the consolidated data of N.V. Philips' Gloeilampenfabricken and those of the United States Philips Trust.

Principles of Valuation

Property, Plant and Equipment

These assets and their depreciation are valued on the basis of replacement value. Changes in the replacement value are credited or charged to Revaluation Surplus.

Intangible Assets

Intangible assets are shown in the balance sheet at no value.

Investments in Non-Consolidated Subsidiaries

Non-consolidated investments are valued at their net tangible asset value, determined in accordance with the principles adopted in these annual accounts.

Sundry Non-Current Assets

These assets are valued at purchase price or at estimated realizable value, whichever is the lower.

Stocks

Stocks are valued at replacement value or at estimated realizable value, whichever is the lower. Changes in replacement value are credited or charged to Revaluation Surplus. The provision for the risk of obsolescence is deducted from the total figure for stocks. Profits arising from transactions within the Philips organization are eliminated.

Accounts Receivable

Accounts receivable are shown at nominal value, less the provision for the risk of bad debts.

Liquid Assets

Securities are valued at purchase price or at their listed stock exchange price at the end of the financial year, whichever is the lower. Shares in N.V. Gemeenschappelijk Bezit van Aandeelen Philips' Gloeilampenfabrieken and debentures of N.V. Philips' Gloeilampenfabrieken and of their associated companies are included at par.

Minority Interests

Minority interests in consolidated subsidiaries are valued on the basis of net tangible asset value, determined in accordance with the principles adopted in these annual accounts.

Sundry Provisions

These provisions do not relate to specific assets; they are formed to meet commitments and risks connected with the course of business. Pension provisions are included under this heading at present value.

Long-Term and Current Liabilities

These liabilities are taken up at nominal value.

Replacement Value

The replacement value is determined on the basis of the price trends of the various assets, making use inter alia of indices. Transfers to Revaluation Surplus pursuant to changes in the replacement value are made after deduction of latent tax liabilities.

Foreign Currencies

In the Combined Statement of Financial Position amounts in foreign currency are converted into guilders at the official exchange rate applicable on the balance sheet date, unless circumstances, as, for instance, the trend of the purchasing power of the currency concerned, call for the adoption of a lower rate.

Exchange differences due to the conversion into guilders of property, plant and equipment and stocks are offset against Revaluation Surplus in the relevant country.

Exchange differences due to the conversion in guilders of nominal assets and liabilities are credited or charged to Profit and Loss Account.

In the Combined Statement of Results, sales and income in foreign currencies are converted at the rates applicable in the relevant periods.

The balance of the relevant profit and loss account is converted at the end of the year at the rates applied in the Combined Statement of Financial Position. The resultant difference is credited or charged to Profit and Loss Account.

Principles of Calculating Profit

- The sales figure represents the net proceeds from goods and services supplied to third parties.
- Depreciation of property, plant and equipment is calculated on the basis of fixed percentages of the replacement value.
- Consumption of raw materials and the other elements in the cost of sales are also calculated on the basis of replacement value.
- Provisions for risks inherent in operations are built up in proportion to the volume of business.
- Expenditure on research, development, patents, licenses, copyrights and concessions is charged in the current year to Profit and Loss Account. Net amounts paid in excess of the net tangible asset value for the acquisition of participations in any year are similarly charged in that year to Profit and Loss Account.

- For taxes on profit, provisions are made on the basis of the profit figure determined in accordance with our principles of valuation, which implies that latent taxes are taken into account. Insofar as the cost of sales differs from historical cost owing to the use of the replacement value, the tax payable on that difference is charged to the provision made for latent taxes at the time of revaluation.

Criteria for Consolidation of Subsidiaries

Companies in which N.V. Philips' Gloeilampenfabrieken or the United States Philips Trust hold, directly or indirectly, more than half of the issued share capital are included in the Combined Statement of Financial Position; the assets and liabilities are then included in full, and minority interests are shown separately in the Statement. A few companies in which the holding is 50% are also consolidated; the assets and liabilities in these cases are included in that proportion. Similar considerations apply to the Combined Statement of Results.

STUDY QUESTIONS FOR CHAPTER 4

1. What effect does inflation have on a firm's financial position and results of operations?
2. What are the basic accounting models for income determination? Which would be your preference? Why?
3. What is the difference between inflation accounting and current value accounting?
4. How does the approach used in continental Europe for inflation accounting differ from the one used in Latin America?
5. What are the prospects for current value accounting being used in the United States? Is there really a need to depart from historical cost accounting, a system which has served the accounting profession well in the past?
6. Can accounting approaches to asset valuation and income determination help to sustain a healthy economy? If so, briefly explain and present an example.
7. How does the Brazilian approach to asset valuation and income determination differ from that used by major companies in the Netherlands?
8. How high must the inflation rate be before a departure from historical cost accounting is justifiable?

9. Given the definition of income as the difference between wealth at two points in time plus consumption and/or dividends, what standards are discussed in the accounting literature for measuring wealth? What effect do these standards have on the determination of income?
10. What are the arguments for and against current value accounting? What progress is being made in different parts of the world to implement various aspects of this concept?
11. What are the arguments for and against price level accounting? What is your opinion on price-level accounting?

ADDITIONAL REFERENCES

1. Accounting Standards Committee. "Statement of Standard Accounting Practice No. 16: Current Cost Accounting." *Accountancy*, April 1980.
2. AlHashim, Dhia D., and Robertson, James W. *Contemporary Issues in Accounting.* Indianapolis, Indiana: Bobbs-Merrill Educational Publishing, 1979, Chapter 3.
3. Arpan, Jeffrey S., and Radebaugh, Lee H. *International Accountng and Multinational Enterprises.* Boston, Massachusetts: Warren, Gorham & Lamont, 1981, Chapter 8.
4. Berliner, Robert W., and Gerboth, Dale L. "FASB Statement No. 33: 'The Great Experiment'." *Journal of Accountancy*, May 1980.
5. Bradford, William D. "Price-Level Restated Accounting and the Measurement of Inflation Gains and Losses." *Accounting Review*, April 1974.
6. Brennan, W. John. "Accounting for Changing Prices: An International Perspective." *Accountant*, 28 April 1977.
7. Burton, John C. "Financial Reporting in an Age of Inflation." *Journal of Accountancy*, February 1975.
8. Chambers, Raymond J. *Accounting Evaluation and Economic Behavior.* Englewood Cliffs, New Jersey: Prentice-Hall, 1965.
9. Choi, Frederick D. S., and Mueller, Gerhard G. *An Introduction to Multinational Accounting.* Englewood Cliffs, New Jersey: Prentice-Hall 1978, Chapter 3.
10. Edwards, Edgar O. "The State of Current Value Accounting." *Accounting Review*, April 1975.
11. Edwards, James Don, and Barrack, John B."Objectives of Financial Statements and Inflation Accounting: A Comparison of Recent

British and American Proposals." *International Journal of Accounting,* Spring 1976.

12. Gynther, R. S. *Accounting for Price-Level Changes: Theory and Procedures.* Oxford: Pergamon Press, Ltd., 1966.
13. Ijiri, Yuji. "The Price-Level Restatement and its Dual Interpretation." *Accounting Review,* April 1976.
14. Noreen, Eric, and Sepe, James. "Market Reactions to Accounting Policy Deliberations: The Inflation Accounting Case." *Accounting Review,* April 1981.
15. Revsine, Lawrence. "The Theory and Measurement of Business Income: A Review Article." *Accounting Review,* April 1981.
16. Rosenfield, Paul. "GPP Accounting-Relevance and Interpretability." *Journal of Accountancy,* August 1975.
17. Rosenfield, Paul. "Current Value Accounting—A Dead End." *Journal of Accountancy,* September 1975.
18. Samuelson, Richard A. "Should Replacement-Cost Changes be Included in Income?" *Accounting Review,* April 1980.
19. Stamp, Edward, and Mason, Alister K. *Asset Valuation and Income Determination: A Consideration of the Alternatives.* Houston, Texas. Scholars Book Co., 1971.
20. Stamp, Edward, and Mason, Alister K. "Current Cost Accounting: British Panacea or Quagmire." *Journal of Accountancy,* April 1977.

Chapter 5

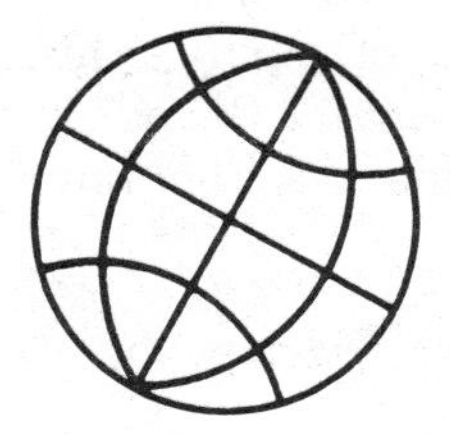

Financial Reporting in Multinational Enterprises

As the international activities of firms increase in size and complexity, so do their financial reporting activities. The number of reports increases because additional groups have a right to, or a need for, information from multinational enterprises (MNEs). The reports grow more complex because there are more complicated transactions and relationships.

For an increasing percentage of multinational firms, foreign investments and international trade represent a significant portion of their total assets and sales. For example, over the last decade U.S. investment abroad grew from $50 billion to $120 billion, and total sales abroad tripled. Both the number of U.S. companies controlling foreign affiliates and the number of these affiliates increased by more than 200%. Such tremendous growth obligates the accounting profession to examine more carefully the operations and reports of MNEs. Because these reports must be prepared to satisfy the needs of different users, there is frequently the need to adjust, translate, aggregate, and disaggregate accounting records prepared on the basis of different accounting standards and in various currencies. From a perspective that considers the needs of different users of reports, this chapter describes four of the major international aspects of financial reporting: changes in currency exchange rates, consolidation, disclosure, and special reports.

GAINS AND LOSSES FROM EXCHANGE RATE CHANGES

Needless to say, one of the most fundamental differences between firms which operate internationally and those which operate only domestically is that the former deal in more than one currency. For example, products of large MNEs, such as IBM, G.E. and Coca-Cola, are sold in more than two-thirds of the world's countries, each of which has its own national currency and currency regulations. Therefore, the MNE records sales in francs, dinars, deutschmarks, rupees, escudos, lira, yen, and so on. Multinationals also have manufacturing plants, sales offices, warehouses, and other operations in foreign countries, and as a result, they have assets, liabilities, equity, and expenses in many different currencies as well. A straightforward question such as "What was the value of the firm's total sales last year?" is relatively simple for a domestic firm to answer, but an MNE cannot simply add francs and pesos and dollars. Rather, it must first convert the sales in different currencies to a single currency. The same problem arises in attempting to answer the question, "What is the total value of the MNE's assets?"

On the surface, it might appear that the conversion problem is fairly simple to solve. All one must do is select one currency to use for reporting (aggregation) purposes, determine the exchange value of each other currency in terms of the selected currency, and multiply the foreign currency denominated sales, assets, or whatever times this exchange rate. For example, let us assume a U.S. firm had sales in France of 2 million French francs, sales in Brazil of 2 million cruzeiros and sales in the United States of $3 million; and let us further assume that the exchange rates were 1 French franc = 25 cents, and 1 cruzeiro = 2 cents. If the U.S. firm reports in dollars, it could compute total sales in this way:

Total Sales	=	*U.S. Sales*	+ *French Sales*	+ *Brazilian Sales*
	=	$3 million	+ [2 million ff × $.25]	+ [2 million cruz × $.02]
	=	$3 million	+ [$500,000]	+ [$40,000]
	=	$3,540,000		

But in reality things would never be so simple, because exchange rates are never static. Exchange rates frequently change. And because they change, conversion values also change, thereby affecting a firm's consolidated income and financial worth.

Suppose for example in the example above the dollar's value rose ten percent relative to both the franc and cruzeiro during the course of the year. Even though sales in francs and cruzeiros were the same, their value in U.S. dollars declines by 10%, computed as follows:

Foreign Sales	=	*French Sales*	+	*Brazilian Sales*
	=	[2 million ff × $.225]	+	[2 million cruz × $.018]
	=	$450,000	+	$36,000
	=	486,000		

The question is, what was the real value of the firm's total sales? If the exchange rates at the beginning of the year are used for conversion, the answer is $3,540,000. If the exchange rates at the end of the year are used, the answer is $3,486,000. Or, if the averages of the exchange rates during the year are used, the answer is $3,513,000. Clearly, the particular exchange rates used affect the dollar value of the firm's global expenses, assets, liabilities, and equity—and the greater the change in the exchange rates, the greater the impact will be.

Still, the subject of exchange rates is far more complex than we have suggested so far. Some countries have more than one official exchange rate at any given moment in time. Some countries have a single official rate, but also a black market rate. In the first case, governments can assign one exchange rate for certain types of transactions, and other rates for other types of transactions. For example, to discourage the imports of luxury items, an unfavorable (that is, a high) exchange rate might be set, even as imports of essential raw materials are encouraged by a favorable (that is, a low) exchange rate.[1] In the case of the black market, it evolves when one cannot obtain foreign currency at the official exchange rate, such as when the government will not approve the

[1]As an illustration, consider a person who wants to import $10,000 of needed machinery and a $10,000 luxury car. To obtain the dollar needed to pay the U.S. exporter, he goes to the bank to exchange his local currency (LC) for dollars. To import the car, he's told the exchange rate is $1 = 5 LC, so he gives up 50,000 LC to buy the car. To import the machinery, he's told the exchange rate is $1 = 1LC, so he has to give up only 10,000 LC to buy the machinery. In this manner, the government discourages the importation of a luxury item by making the buyer spend more local currency.

transaction for whatever reason. In either of these situations, a firm has several possible *types* of exchange rates to select from, as well as the changes in their values over time!

Finally, changes in the exchange rates can cause gains and losses for the firm. For example, in 1975 Dow Chemical reported a foreign exchange gain of over $20 million, and Exxon one of over $215 million. In the very next year, Dow reported a foreign exchange loss of $40 million. Exxon in the meantime reported a far less dramatic gain of $60 million. Still, not all of these gains and losses were "realized," that is, actually incurred as one currency was exchanged for another. Some were "unrealized" because no actual exchange of currencies took place—they resulted simply from *translating* (restating) accounts that were denominated in foreign currencies into dollars.[2] Therefore, the attempt to report the exact value of the results of operations has another level of complexity, for some gains and losses are recognized and realized while others are recognized but not realized. All of this sounds confusing because it *is* confusing. To help diminish the confusion, we will now shift to a more specific explanation of the actual treatment of the gains and losses from changes in exchange rates. Our discussion is divided into two parts: transaction (that is, realized) gains and losses, and translation (or unrealized) gains and losses.

Calculating Transaction Gains and Losses

If exchange rates change between the time when a transaction is initially recorded (booked) and when it is finally settled, a transaction gain or loss is incurred. For example, suppose a U.S. firm purchases machinery from a British supplier for £100,000 on an account at a time when the exchange rate is £1 = $1.80. The transaction is recorded on the U.S. books as follows:

Purchases	$180,000	
Accounts Payable		$180,000

Thirty days later, when the U.S. purchaser gets ready to settle the accounts payable, the exchange rate has changed to £1=$1.70. Therefore only $170,000 is necessary to obtain the £100,000 owed the British supplier, rather than the $180,000 originally booked. Hence, there is a transaction *gain* of $10,000. Of course, if the exchange rate had moved

[2]For example, inventories, cash, and short-term debt.

in the other direction, say to £ = $1.90, there would have been a transaction *loss* of $10,000.

As the example shows, the gain or loss is calculated by determining the impact of any difference in the exchange rate between the day that the transaction is initially recorded and the day that it is settled. (The specific daily exchange rates are called the "spot rates"—the rates currently in force on any given day.) Still, how should the final settlement in the example above be recorded on the books of the U.S. firm?

The first approach, referred to as the "one-transaction perspective," would show the final settlement in this manner:

Accounts Payable	$180,000	
Cash		$170,000
Purchases		$ 10,000

To record the settlement of the liability to the British supplier, with a favorable exchange adjustment recognized by a reduction in the cost of purchases.

The one-transaction approach considers the transaction (in this case, acquiring an asset) as not being complete until the final settlement is made. Therefore, recording an asset at the date of purchase is considered as only one step towards the completion of the purchase transaction. If the exchange rate has changed as of the date of the final cash settlement, the exchange adjustment is considered as an adjustment of the original cost of the asset acquired, but *not* as an exchange gain or loss.

The second approach is called the "two-transaction perspective." According to this approach, there are two distinct transactions: in the above example, the purchase of an asset and the assumption of a foreign exchange risk. Those who hold this view argue that delaying payment of an asset denominated in a foreign currency should not affect the cost of the asset acquired. Rather, any loss or gain from the delay in payment should be treated as a cost or return for assuming the risk of fluctuating exchange rates. Therefore, the two-transaction approach would record the cash settlement of the above example as follows:

Accounts Payable	$180,000	
Cash		$170,000
Exchange Adjustment: Gain		$ 10,000

To record settlement of the liability to the British supplier, with a favorable exchange adjustment recognized by a gain to be closed in the Income Summary account.

There is no clear global consensus as to which approach is better. Therefore, some countries require the one-transaction perspective, others the two-transaction perspective, and others leave it to the discretion of the firms themselves. In the United States, FASB supports the two-transaction perspective, and requires the immediate recognition of gains or losses from transactions denominated in foreign currencies. These gains and losses are considered normal operating items on the income statement. (As we will point out later, however, FASB treats non-transaction (translation) gains and losses differently, that is, as adjustments to the stockholders' equity account). In most other countries, gains and losses from foreign currency payables and receivables are deferred until the transactions are completed. And when the transactions are settled, many countries still do not take the resulting gain or loss to the income statement.

Accounting for transactions denominated in foreign currencies becomes even more complicated when a firm attempts to protect itself from exchange rate fluctuations. In the case above, for example, the firm could enter into a "forward contract" to buy British pounds at a specified rate called the "forward rate." A forward contract is simply an agreement upon the exchange rate, an agreement made by a person who wants to sell a certain amount of currency in the future and a person who wants to buy that amount of currency in the future. As an addition to the case we have been considering, perhaps there is a British firm that wants to purchase a U.S. tractor in thirty days; therefore the firm will need a certain amount of dollars. Our U.S. firm buying British machinery, on the other hand, needs to exchange dollars for pounds in thirty days to pay the British machinery supplier (who is not necessarily, or even likely to be, the company purchasing the tractor). Therefore, the firm that wants to exchange pounds for dollars in thirty days (our U.S. firm) tries to find one that wants to exchange dollars for pounds in thirty days (the British firm buying an American Tractor). These two can then sign a contract to exchange pounds and dollars at an agreed upon rate, no matter what the spot rate is thirty days in the future. It is this agreed upon rate that is called the forward rate.

Though there is certainly additional work involved in entering into a forward contract, it does eliminate the risk of (and potential loss from) any changes in the exchange rate. As you recall in our first formulation of the British machinery example, the U.S. purchaser experienced a gain because the dollar strengthened against the pound. However, had the dollar weakened, the American firm would have experienced a loss. Thus, to eliminate any possibility of such a loss, the firm could enter into a forward contract to buy pounds at a forward rate of *no greater than £1 = $1.80*. Some specifics will make the virtues of this contract apparent.

If the firm enters into the forward contract with a forward rate of £1 = $1.80, in thirty days it gives $180,000 to the forward contract supplier and receives £100,000. It then uses these £100,000 to pay the British machinery supplier. Suppose the firm had not entered into this forward contract, and the spot rate on the day of final settlement had gone to £1 = $1.90; the firm would have had to pay $190,000 to obtain the £100,000 necessary to pay the British machinery supplier. Thus using a forward contract eliminated an exchange rate loss.

Needless to say, though, the forward contract works both ways. If the spot rate on the day of settlement had moved to £1 = $1.70, then, for the American firm, having entered into a forward contract at £1 = $1.80 would *not* end up being a good decision, because it is obligated to exchange $180,000 for £100,000 according to the terms of the forward contract. If it had not entered into the forward contract, the American firm could have exchanged only $170,000 for the £100,000 it needed. Unfortunately, there is no sure way for a firm to know beforehand whether or not it is wise to enter into a forward contract. Only after one knows what the spot rate actually was on the day of final settlement can this assessment be made. It's a gamble either way—but at least a forward contract contributes stability to the international purchase because the exact terms of the exchange are known in advance.

Due to the great complexities of the accounting procedures for forward contracts, they will not be discussed here. For more information about them, the reader can refer to FAS #52 or the relevant chapter in any recent international accounting textbook. Before we conclude this section on transactions, though, we should emphasize that the accounting complexities we have discussed here arise only for transactions denominated in *foreign* currencies. That is, if a U.S. firm is able to denominate all foreign sales and purchases in U.S. dollars, it will not expose itself to any transaction gains or losses from changes in exchange rates, and therefore, it will not need the special accounting procedures related to such changes. Thus, in the machinery example above, if the British machinery supplier is willing to accept payment in dollars, then the U.S. firm does not risk any gain or loss from a change in the exchange rate. Purchases and accounts payable are initially booked at $180,000, and at final settlement, accounts payable is debited by $180,000 and the cash account credited for $180,000. In this case, the foreign exchange risk is assumed by the British exporter. Naturally, while this arrangement is ideal for the U.S. purchaser, it is not always possible, since the foreign supplier may not be willing to accept payment in dollars.

Translation Gains and Losses

Accounting for translation gains and losses is even more complicated than accounting for transaction gains and losses.

Foreign currency translation gains and losses are a product of the consolidation process. Hence, unlike transaction gains and loses, there is no actual transaction: no particular currency is actually exchanged for another. Thus, the translation process is not a valuation process, but rather a restatement (that is, putting one currency in the terms of another). One would not expect, then, to reach the value of assets and liabilities in dollars through the process of translation.

The U.S. Financial Accounting Standards Board states that the translation of the financial statements of an enterprise should accomplish the following objectives:

1. To provide information that is generally compatible with the expected economic effects of a rate change on an enterprise's cash flows and equity.
2. To present the consolidated financial statements of an enterprise in conformity with U.S. generally accepted accounting principles.
3. To reflect in consolidated financial statements the financial results and relationships of the individual consolidated entities as measured in their functional currencies.[3]

Four different translation methods have been utilized in practice throughout the world: the current–noncurrent method, the monetary–nonmonetary method, the temporal method, and the current rate method.

[3]Financial Accounting Standards Board, Statement 52, "Foreign Currency Translation," ¶ 70.

THE METHODS OF TRANSLATION

The Current–Noncurrent Method

The current–noncurrent method of translation emphasizes the balance sheet classifications of "current" and "noncurrent" items. In translating foreign financial statements, the current exchange rate (at the date of closing) is applied to current assets and liabilities, while the historical exchange rates in effect when the transactions occurred are applied to the noncurrent assets, liabilities, and stockholders' equity accounts of the foreign entity. Income statement items are translated at an average rate, except for those items which are related to assets and liabilities translated at historical exchange rates (for example, depreciation).

The current–noncurrent method of translating foreign financial statements was supported in the U.S. Accounting Research Bulletin No. 43 (Chapter 12) and in the U.S. Accounting Principles Board Opinion No. 6 (¶ 18). The method has been criticized, however, for its emphasis on the balance sheet classifications which the method's critics see as irrelevant to the objective of translation. An example of this deficiency would be translating inventory and long-term liabilities where the measurement bases do not coincide with the balance sheet classifications. The U.S. dollar devaluations of 1971 and 1973, and the change in the foreign exchange market from fixed to floating rates, necessitated reconsidering what accounting method should be used in translating foreign financial statements.

The Monetary–Nonmonetary Method

Like the current–noncurrent method of translation, the monetary–nonmonetary method also emphasizes characteristics of the balance sheet items, but reclassifies these items into monetary items (assets and liabilities with fixed monetary amounts) and nonmonetary items (all other assets, liabilities, and stockholders' equity accounts). Monetary items are translated at the current exchange rate, nonmonetary items at their historical exchange rates. Income statement items are translated at an average rate except for those income statement items related to the assets and liabilities translated at historical rates.

If the nonmonetary items of the foreign entity are stated at prices other than those at historical cost, the monetary–nonmonetary method produces unreasonable results. Applying historical rates for nonmonetary items which are stated at current market prices, for example, would produce questionable results. Instead, it seems that the measurement bases of nonmonetary items should determine the appropriate exchange rates to be used in translating these items from a foreign currency to U.S. dollars. This means that the monetary–nonmonetary method does not provide a comprehensive method of translation.

Most of the CPA firms in the U.S. and the AICPA have supported the monetary–nonmonetary method on the assumption that it is consistent with the historical-cost accounting generally accepted in the U.S. The monetary–nonmonetary method has also found support in other parts of the world and is used by most Latin American countries.

The Temporal Method

The temporal method translates assets and liabilities based on their individual attributes. This method, which retains the measurement bases of foreign financial statements items, has the singularly attractive feature of being able to accommodate any basis of measurement (for example, historical cost, or replacement cost). Lorensen states:

> Since translation is a measurement conversion process, it cannot change any of the accounting principles used in preparing the foreign money financial statements other than the unit of measurement. Changing any other principle—for example, changing assets stated at historical cost to assets stated at replacement price—is a separate process. Translation is justified by the need to use a single unit of measure in consolidated financial statements. Changing any other principle is not translation and must be justified on other grounds.[4]

FASB Statement No. 8 supported the temporal method, calling it a

> . . . more generally valid method for achieving the objective of translation. It provides a conceptual basis for the procedures that are now used to apply the monetary–nonmonetary method.[5]

In applying this method, income statement items are translated at an average rate except for those items related to assets and liabilities translated at historical rates.

[4]Leonard Lorenson, *Reporting Foreign Operations of U.S. Companies in U.S. Dollars,* Accounting Research Study No. 12 (New York: AICPA, 1972).

[5]Financial Accounting Standards Board, *Accounting for the Translation of Foreign Currency Transactions and Foreign Currency Financial Statements,* Statement No. 8, (Stamford, Connecticut: FASB, October 1975), ¶ 124.

The Current Rate Method

Proponents of the current rate method reject the other methods of translation because they are done on an "as if" basis, that is, as if the foreign-based operations had been conducted in the parent company's environment. To present fairly the foreign-based operations, they argue, it is imperative that the translation should be directed toward showing the relationships that exist in those foreign environments. Thus, the translation process should preserve both the relationships (that is, the financial ratios) in the foreign financial statements and the underlying accounting standards used in their preparation. Generally speaking, based on the current rate method, all balance sheet and income statement items are translated at the current exchange rate.

In support of the current rate method of translation, Parkinson states:

> It is not really the individual assets and liabilities that are at risk in a foreign operation; rather, it is the entire business that is at risk. The business is conducted entirely in a foreign environment and future cash flows will be in a foreign currency. Future operating results can be measured in a meaningful way in . . . dollars only if all future revenues and costs (including costs carried forward from a previous period) are translated at current exchange rates.[6]

Comparisons

Exhibit 5.1 summarizes the specific exchange rates used for various balance sheet categories in each translation method. Apart from any theoretical differences, a legitimate question can be asked: What *real* difference does the use of a particular translation method make? To partially answer this question, Exhibit 5.2 shows the effect of the different translation methods on the balance sheet of a hypothetical firm, assuming that the current exchange rate is 50% of the historical exchange rate. The translated value of total assets ranges from a low of $900 under the current rate method to a high of $1,700 under the monetary–nonmonetary method (due primarily to the difference in the translated value of fixed assets). Another more detailed example of the real impact of different translation methods—this time on a firm's income statement—is provided by Exhibit 5.3 (pp. 134–35). Note the dif-

---

[6]R. MacDonald Parkinson, *Translation of Foreign Currencies* (Toronto: Canadian Institute of Chartered Accountants, 1972), p. 94.

ference in net earnings before tax, and the fact that the temporal method results in a $20,000 foreign exchange loss while the current rate method resulted in a $74,250 foreign exchange gain (obviously influencing the earnings before and after tax).

EXHIBIT 5.1 *Exchange Rates Used to Translate Selected Assets and Liabilities*

	Current-Noncurrent	*Monetary-Nonmonetary*	*Current Rate*	*Temporal*
Cash, current receivables and payables	C	C	C	C
Inventory	C	H	C	C or H
Fixed assets	H	H	C	H
Long-term receivables and payables	H	C	C	C

NOTE: C = current exchange rate, H = historical exchange rate.

EXHIBIT 5.2 *Balance Sheet Effect of Translation*

	Local Currency	*Current-Noncurrent*	*Monetary-Nonmonetary*	*Current Rate*
Cash	LC100	$ 100*	$ 100*	$100*
Inventory	200	200*	400†	200*
Fixed assets	600	1,200†	1,200†	600*
Totals	LC900	$1,500	$1,700	$900
Current liabilities	LC250	250*	250*	250*
Long-term debt	150	300†	150*	150*
Net worth	500	950	1,300	500
Totals	LC900	$1,500	$1,700	$900

NOTE: Net worth is a plug figure.
*Translated at the current rate of 1LC = $1.
†Translated at the historical rate of 1LC = $2.
SOURCE: Jeffrey S. Arpan and Lee H. Radebaugh, *International Accounting and Multinational Enterprises* (N.Y.: John Wiley & Sons, Inc., 1981), p. 106. © 1981 by John Wiley & Sons, Inc. Used with permission.

Popularity of the Current Rate Method

The current rate method for translation has been the most widely practiced method throughout the world, and until the passage of FAS #52, the United States was one of only a few industrialized countries that required some other method (FAS #8 required the temporal method). The passage of FAS #52 now has the United States primarily using the current rate method, although it still allows firms to use the temporal method under certain conditions.

Furthermore, the International Accounting Standards Committee (IASC) also has moved toward requiring the use of the current rate method. In December of 1977, the IASC issued Exposure Draft 11 requiring the use of either the temporal or the current rate method for translating foreign financial statements.[7] Then the IASC delayed the process of issuing a definitive standard on this issue in order to gain from the experiences of various countries that were using different translation methods. Finally, a revised draft was issued on August 31, 1982 by the IASC, Exposure Draft 23, requiring the use of the current exchange rate in translating the financial statements of those foreign-based operations not considered to be an integral part of the parent company's operations and whose transactions in general have no effect on the cash flow of the parent company. Any exchange adjustments (that is, gains or losses) resulting from this process are to be regarded as stockholders' equity items and shown on the balance sheet. If, however, foreign-based operations *are* an integral part of the parent company's operations, any exchange adjustments resulting from translation are to be regarded as income statement items. Generally speaking, European and Asian countries have supported for some time the use of the current rate method of translation. Thus, the change in the IASC's position was at least partially attributable to the change in the position of the U.S. Financial Accounting Standard Board in 1981.

In 1981, FASB changed its position of support from the monetary–nonmonetary method to the current rate method in its Statement No. 52:

> All elements of financial statements shall be translated by using a *current exchange rate.* For assets and liabilities, the exchange rate at the balance

[7]International Accounting Standards Committee, *Accounting for Foreign Transaction and Translation of Foreign Financial Statements*, Exposure Draft 11 (London: IASC, December 1, 1977), paragraph 17.

EXHIBIT 5.3 *Statement of Income and Retained Earnings*

		Temporal		*Current Rate*	
	Local Currency	*Exchange Rate*	*U.S. Dollars*	*Exchange Rate*	*U.S. Dollars*
Sales	1,400,000	$2.07 *	$2,898,000	2.07	$2,898,000
Cost of goods sold					
Beginning inventory	275,000	2.03 **	558,250	2.04 §§	561,000
Purchases	450,000	2.06 †	927,000	2.07	931,500
	725,000		1,485,250		1,492,500
Ending inventory	250,000	2.08	520,000	2.10	525,000
Cost of materials	475,000		965,250		967,500
Labor	400,000	2.07	828,000	2.07	828,000
Depreciation	90,000	1.97	177,300	2.07	186,300
Total cost of goods sold	965,000		1,970,550		1,981,800
Selling and administrative expenses	150,000	2.07	310,500	2.07	310,500
Foreign exchange loss (gain)	—		20,000		(74,250)
	1,115,000		2,301,050		2,218,050

Earnings before taxes	285,000		596,950		679,950
Taxes on income	170,000	2.07	351,900	2.07	351,900
Earnings after tax	115,000		245,050		328,050
Beginning retained earnings	150,000		295,950		295,950
Net earnings	115,000		245,050		328,050
	265,000		541,000		624,000
Less dividends	90,000	2.10	189,000	2.10	189,000
Ending retained earnings	175,000		$ 352,000		$ 435,000

NOTE: Assume that taxes were paid throughout the year and that dividends were declared at the end of the year. Also, the beginning retained earnings balance came from the previous year's statement.

* The average rate during the year.

** The average rate during which beginning inventory was accumulated.

†The average rate during which inventory purchases were made.

§§The rate at the beginning of the year.

SOURCE: Jeffrey S. Arpan and Lee H. Radebaugh, *International Accounting and Multinational Enterprises* (N.Y.: John Wiley & Sons, Inc., 1981), p. 112.

sheet date shall be used. For revenues, expenses, gains, and losses, the exchange rate at the dates on which those elements are recognized shall be used. Because translation at the exchange rates at the dates the numerous revenues, expenses, gains, and losses are recognized is generally impractical, an appropriately weighted average exchange rate for the period may be used to translate those elements.[8]

The position of FASB on the translation process, based on Statement No. 52, can be summarized as follows:

1. Before translation, foreign financial statements should be prepared in conformity with U.S. generally accepted accounting standards applied in terms of the functional currency in which the entity primarily conducts its business, generates and expends cash, reinvests cash, or converts and distributes cash to its parent.
2. All assets and liabilities of a foreign entity are translated from its functional currency into the reporting currency at the current exchange rate.
3. All revenues, expenses, gains, and losses of a foreign entity are translated from its functional currency into the reporting currency at the weighted average exchange rate for the period.
4. Exchange adjustments (translation adjustments, or gains or losses) which result from the translation of the foreign entity's financial statements are deferred in a separate stockholders' equity account called "accumulated translation adjustment."
5. Exchange adjustments (transaction gains or losses) which result from foreign currency transactions (transactions denominated in a currency other than the entity's functional currency) are, generally speaking, recognized in the income of the period in which the exchange rate changes.
6. *Transaction gains and losses* on the following should be deferred and reported as *translation adjustments:*
   a. Foreign currency transactions that are considered as effective economic hedges against a net investment in a foreign entity.
   b. Foreign currency long-term intercompany transactions.
   c. Foreign currency transactions that are considered as effective economic hedges against firm and identifiable foreign currency commitments.
7. The accumulated translation adjustment account is not realized un-

[8]Financial Accounting Standards Board, Statement 52, ¶ 12.

til the sale or substantially complete liquidation of the net investment in the foreign entity takes place.

8. If the cumulative inflation rate in a country over a three-year period approximates more than 100%, the currency of a foreign entity cannot be considered as stable enough to serve as a functional currency. In this case, the financial statements of this foreign entity should be remeasured into the functional currency of the reported enterprise (for example, the parent company). For this highly inflationary environment, the remeasurement process required by Statement No. 52 is similar to that required by Statement No. 8, except for both the deferred income taxes and the life insurance policy acquisition costs, which are translated using the current exchange rate.
9. The current exchange rate is the rate applicable to dividend remittances, because cash flows to the parent company from the foreign entity can be converted at only this rate. In addition, realization of net investments in foreign entities is usually done through the cash flows from those entities.
10. For purposes of applying Statement No. 52, if the foreign entity's accounting period ends at a date different than that of the parent company, the current exchange rate used in the translation process is the rate in effect at the end of the accounting period of the foreign entity.
11. Stockholders' equity accounts are translated as follows:
    a. Capital accounts are translated at historical exchange rates.
    b. The retained earnings account is translated by adding to the translated amount of this account, as of the end of the prior period, the translated amount of income for the current period, and then deducting from the total the translated amount of dividends declared during the current accounting period.
12. If a foreign entity's books of record are not maintained in its functional currency, financial statements of this foreign entity should be measured into the functional currency prior to translation. The resulting gains or losses out of this remeasurement should be recognized currently in the income of the foreign entity.

How to Report Gains and Losses

The U.S. method of translation in FASB Statement No. 8 required the immediate recognition of *all* foreign currency exchange gains or losses, a treatment of the exchange adjustment that came under attack from the business community for many reasons. For example, it was argued that in an environment of floating currencies and fluctuating exchange rates, the immediate recognition of *all* exchange gains and losses caused erratic changes in the reported results of operations of companies with significant international activities, especially for interim periods. In addition, some authorities contended that the immediate recognition of *all* exchange adjustments would incline companies toward uneconomic actions so that they could protect themselves from exchange exposure.

There are many examples of managerial decisions influenced by exchange adjustments. Major multinational corporations—such as ITT—hedging their commitments and incurring large costs in the process are examples of uneconomic decisions that the top management of such corporations must make to protect themselves against accounting (that is, foreign exchange) exposures. Other examples of how management decisions are affected by accounting results can be seen in the actions of corporations like R.J. Reynolds Industries, which refinanced its foreign debts with U.S. dollar Euronotes and in the process incurred prepayment penalties.

Proponents of the immediate recognition of *all* exchange gains or losses feel that rate changes are historical in character and that, as such, the resulting gains or losses should be reported currently on income statements. Based on this view, the deferral of exchange adjustments to smooth the reported incomes would be undesirable.

In its new standard, FAS #52, FASB decided to change its previous stand on this issue and adopted a compromise position. Companies can now defer part of the exchange adjustments (that is, the translation adjustments related to the translation of the foreign entity's financial statements) and report that portion as a stockholders' equity account. They can recognize the other part of the exchange adjustments (that is, the transaction gains and losses resulting from foreign currency transactions) in the current income of the period in which the exchange rate changes.

In other English-speaking countries there are some similarities. The Institute of Chartered Accountants of Scotland recommends that exchange adjustments resulting from the exchange rate change on fixed assets and long-term liabilities be considered as adjustments to stockholders' equity.[9] The Accounting Standards Committee of the United

[9]Institute of Chartered Accountants of Scotland, "Treatment in Company Accounts of Changes in the Exchange Rates of International Currencies," *The Accountant's Magazine* (September 1970), ¶ 40.

Kingdom, in its many pronouncements, favors only treating gains and losses that result from the translation of fixed assets as a part of stockholders' equity, whereas gains or losses that result from net borrowings are to be considered as a part of income for the accounting period.[10] In addition, Parkinson, mentioned earlier (p. 131), believes that exchange adjustments pertaining to those changes in the exchange rates which are likely to reverse in the foreseeable future should be deferred and amortized over a lengthy period.[11] We might conclude by mentioning incidentally that the IASC takes a position similar to FASB's.

CONSOLIDATION PROBLEMS

The treatment of the foreign exchange gains and losses from translations is clearly a major problem of consolidation for MNEs, but it is certainly not the only one, or even the major one. The MNE faces other major problems, such as whether or not to consolidate and if so, by what method; how to assuage the underlying differences in the various accounting procedures the MNE confronts; and how to eliminate intracorporate profits.

To Consolidate or Not to Consolidate

It may surprise some readers that the preparation of consolidated financial reports is *not* a common practice worldwide. In fact, in some countries, such as Colombia, consolidated financial reports are *prohibited* by law, and in most countries they are the exception rather than the rule. Nor is this worldwide tendency limited only to the consolidation of foreign operations with domestic operations. For in many countries, financial reports do not even consolidate *domestic* subsidiaries—a phenomenon known as "parent company only" financial reports.

Generally, financial reports are consolidated because the consolidation is either required by law or is the "generally accepted" practice. In the United States, for example, the global consolidation of tax reports is required by U.S. tax law because the United States taxes the world-

[10] For example, Accounting Standards Committee, *Foreign Currency Transactions*, Proposed Statement of Accounting Practice-ED21 (London: ASC, 6 October 1977).

[11] R. MacDonald Parkinson, *Translation of Foreign Currencies* (Toronto: Canadian Institute of Chartered Accountants, 1972), p. 102.

wide income of U.S. firms. The same is true for Canada, West Germany, and the U.K. On the other hand, the global consolidation of corporate financial reports (or annual reports) is practiced in the United States because it is a "generally accepted accounting procedure." In other countries where the consolidation of financial reports is practiced, it is generally required by law. Germany, Japan, and the U.K. have such laws. Note that without the law requiring consolidation, there is little incentive for most firms to prepare consolidated financial statements, since consolidation takes considerable time, effort, and money. It also provides more information about a company's financial position than many firms wish to have known.

Thus, for many countries, the global consolidation of financial and/or tax statements is neither required nor commonly practiced. U.S. firms, however, have no option to consolidate or not to consolidate. They must. Their only options concern *how*.

U.S. Methods of Consolidation

On a parent company's statement, subsidiaries and affiliates are carried as investments. Income from their operations is recognized either when it is earned—the equity method—or when it is received as a dividend—the cost method.

The cost method can be used only when the U.S. parent owns less than 20% of the affiliate's voting stock and when the initial acquisition was accounted for by the purchase method. When a dividend is received, the parent's books record the dividend income, but there is no change in the carried value of the investment.

Under the equity method, the income from foreign operations increases the investment by the parent in the foreign affiliate, and the dividends from the affiliate reduce the investment account. Therefore, in the equity method income is recognized by the parent when it is earned by the affiliate, not when it is declared as a dividend.

The following example illustrates the different accounting treatments of affiliate income. If a wholly owned foreign subsidiary earns income that is the equivalent of $1 million, the equity method debits the "investment in subsidiary" account by $1 milion, and credits the "equity in subsidiary income" account by $1 million. If the cost method is used (that is, the parent owns less than 20% of the stock), no entries would be made because no dividends are received. If the wholly owned subsidiary pays a dividend to the parent of, say, $500,000, under the equity method the parent would debit the dividends receivable account by $500,000 and credit the "investment in subsidiary" account by $500,000. Under the cost method, the entry would be to credit dividend income instead.

So much for the parent's statement, but what about the consolidated statement? As shown in Exhibit 5.4, in consolidated statements affiliates are still carried as investments; thus income is recognized by the cost or the equity method, depending on the parent's percentage of ownership, just as in the parent's statements. For subsidiaries however, the investment account is eliminated and the financial statements of the parent and all subsidiaries are added together *line by line* to form the consolidated statement.

To illustrate these differences, assume a foreign operation has income in its own currency equal to $1 million, and the U.S. parent has income of $10 million. On a consolidated basis, the parent if it owns more than 50% of the foreign operation would eliminate the investment in the subsidiary account and would add to its own income the appropriate percentage of the foreign operation's income. Thus, if it owns 100% of the subsidiary it adds the full $1 million; if it owns 55%, it adds $550,000. If the parent owns between 20 and 50%, the investment in the affiliate account would not be eliminated, but would be increased by the appropriate percentage of income earned by the affiliate attributable to the parent. Thus, if the parent owns 25%, its investment account in the consolidated statements increases by $250,000. Finally, if the parent owns less than 20%, the investment in the affiliate account is neither eliminated nor changed in amount regardless of the foreign affiliate's income.

Restatement of Accounts

Line-by-line consolidation obviously requires all subsidiary balance sheets and income statements to be restated in dollars. It may also require

EXHIBIT 5.4 *Recognition of Subsequent Activity*

	Parent Statements	*Consolidated Statements*
Subsidiary	Equity	Line by line
Affiliate ≥ 20% but ≤ 50%	Equity	Equity
Affiliate < 20%	Cost	Cost

all of the underlying accounting procedures used to value the accounts to be the same. For a U.S. firm, this means restating foreign financial statements into U.S. GAAP. The restatement into dollars converts all the currencies into one currency so that the results of operations can be added. The restatement of all accounts into U.S. GAAP converts different kinds of accounting practices and procedures into a single type.

For U.S. MNEs the currency restatement must be done according to FAS #52, as described earlier. The restatement into GAAP is even more complex, and many of the related problems have already been discussed in Chapter 4. But to refresh your memory, consider a few examples.

First, the consolidation of inventory. In some countries, direct costing of inventories is either permitted or required, but it is prohibited in the U.S. Therefore, foreign inventories valued at direct cost must be restated to conform with U.S. GAAP. Second, in some countries, such as Italy for example, corporate contributions to political parties are legal expenses, but these are illegal in the U.S. Therefore, such expenses claimed in Italy cannot be consolidated with the U.S. parent's expenses, and the reported Italian income would have to be adjusted upward (because expenses were overstated, from the American perspective, by the deduction of any political contribution expense). Finally, consider the issue of inflation adjustments. For whose inflation rate should the consolidated statements be adjusted? Should the foreign statements be adjusted first for their local inflation rate and then translated into dollars, or should unadjusted foreign statements be translated into dollars first and then adjusted for the U.S. inflation rate? The answer is, in a way, both. According to FAS #33, the constant dollar supplement requires the "translate then adjust" method, while the current cost supplement requires the "adjust then translate" method.

Generally, to keep from having to restate all foreign accounts into U.S. GAAP, many firms find it easier to maintain two sets of local financial records. One set is kept according to local accounting procedures, and the other according to U.S. GAAP. Therefore, in the inventory example above, inventory accounts in the first set of books could be valued at direct cost, while those in the U.S. GAAP version of the local books would not. While keeping multiple records may seem expensive and cumbersome, it is a common practice even for purely domestic U.S. firms: there are tax books, financial reporting books, and internal management books. But for a U.S. multinational, it is even more essential, for they have *at least* a dual compliment of multiple records—one set for the parent, one set for each subsidiary, and a consolidated set. Obviously, to keep such multiple records requires a rather elaborate internal information system, a subject to be discussed in Chapter 6.

Elimination of Intercorporate Transactions

Another aspect of consolidation involves the elimination of intercorporate transactions. While intercorporate receivables and payables, security holdings, purchases, interest, and dividends must all be eliminated, the most intricate part of the process involves intercorporate profits.

In both domestic and multinational firms, the term *intercorporate profit* refers to profit arising from the transfer of inventories, properties, or other assets (1) between companies included in consolidated financial statements, (2) between such companies and investee companies accounted for under the equity method, and (3) between investee companies accounted for under the equity method. Such transfers will arise because members of a corporate family usually perform certain activities for each other. For example, in a vertically integrated, multinational aluminum firm, its mining subsidiary in Jamaica may mine bauxite and sell it to a U.S. smelting subsidiary, which then sells the aluminum ingots to a German rolling mill subsidiary, which then sells the sheet aluminum to a French fabricating subsidiary, which sells it to the European marketing subsidiary, which finally sells it to European customers. At each point, an intercorporate transfer (a sale) occurs, generally with some profit accruing to each seller. Although in each situation profit is properly recorded in the financial records of the selling company, from a consolidated viewpoint a profit cannot be recognized until it is confirmed by a sale to some customer *outside* the consolidated entity. Therefore, the general purpose of eliminating intercorporate profits in consolidated statements is to exclude from the consolidation the profit or loss, net of taxes, arising from transactions within the consolidated firm, and correspondingly to reduce the carried amount of assets remaining in the consolidated entity. In most cases, the gross profit of the selling company is used.

The current practice for most U.S. companies in accounting for majority owned subsidiaries in consolidation under the equity method is as follows:[12]

[12]Source: G. Watt, R. Hammer, and M. Burge, *Accounting for the Multinational Corporation*, Financial Executives Research Foundation, New York, 1977, pp. 34–35.

1. When profit arises from a sale by the parent to a subsidiary, the entire profit is eliminated by a charge to the parent interest.
2. When a profit arises from a sale by a subsidiary to the parent, the entire profit is eliminated either by (a) charging the profit eliminated entirely to the parent interest (the parent's share is charged to consolidated income and the minority's share to its balance sheet), or by (b) charging the profit eliminated *pro rata* to the parent and minority interests.

A "partial" elimination procedure is generally followed for less than majority-owned affiliates accounted for under the equity method. Profit is normally eliminated by the parent on a sale to the affiliate only to the extent of the parent's ownership interest in the affiliate.

What makes this profit elimination process complicated for an MNE is the volume and the complexity of international transfers. There are tariffs and other import duties, export credits, changes in the exchange rates, different tax rates in the buying and selling countries, and so on. The actual entries for eliminating intercorporate profits, as a result, are also very complex—in fact, too complex for the purposes of this book.[13] However, one should recognize that in countries not requiring a consolidated statement, intercorporate profits are *not* eliminated. A not infrequent practice in such countries is to show intercorporate profits in the parent's books (thereby overstating the parent's real profit) and at the same time to hide intercorporate losses in the books of the unconsolidated subsidiaries.

Finally, even more important than the actual process of eliminating intercorporate profits is the financial and competitive impact resulting from intercorporate transactions. By altering intercorporate shipments—and their prices—income can be moved around the world to countries with lower tax rates. Similarly, a host of government policies and regulations can be circumvented or lessened in impact. These issues are discussed in greater detail in Chapter 6, but for the moment they lead us quite naturally into the whole subject of how financial information is and should be disclosed.

DISCLOSURE

The disclosure of information is a highly controversial subject in financial reporting. For reasons already alluded to earlier in this chapter,

[13]For a more comprehensive treatment of intercorporate profit elimination procedures, see Watt, Hammer, and Burge, *op. cit.*, as well as *Accounting Research Bulletin No. 51.*

users of financial statements generally desire more disclosure than firms prefer to make. Good economic decision making requires adequate and appropriate information—this is the user's perspective. On the other hand, economic and political entities do not always want to have informed users of their information. Sometimes information too easily can be misinterpreted or misused; other times, companies would simply prefer to conceal information about certain activities. That is not to imply that companies might have poor or illegal motives for such secretive tendencies. For example, it might behoove a company to keep it from general knowledge (that is, from its competition) how much it is spending on research and development.

Disclosure is an especially fraught and complex issue for MNEs because their financial statements have so many more users, and, some cynics have argued, because MNEs engage in more questionable activities. Therefore, we will devote the rest of this chapter to exploring the disclosure issue, with an emphasis on segment reporting, the inclusion of forecasts, and social (and other) "impact" reports. We will close with a few comments about the mechanical problems of financial reporting in general. However, before the discussion of these particular aspects of disclosure begins, a few words are in order about the general levels and patterns of disclosure around the world.

The Reasons for the Patterns of Disclosure Worldwide

In the global patterns of disclosure, perhaps the best known and most often referred to example is Switzerland, not because of its disclosure but rather because of its *lack* of disclosure. The annual reports of some of the large Swiss firms—several of them among the world's largest firms—are studded with glossy photographs interspersed throughout a few thousand words of descriptive, if not flowery narrative, but they contain only a few lines of financial data. Nor do they contain any explanation of the little information that is disclosed or how it is derived. In sharp contrast, the 10-K reports of U.S. multinationals contain pages of financial data and explanatory notes—but no pictures. Yet before the firms and citizens of the U.S. pat themselves on the back too quickly, they should be told that generally Scandinavian and British firms disclose even more information than U.S. firms disclose. In short, the levels of disclosure vary considerably throughout the world for many reasons, some of them good, some of them not good.

In the broadest terms, the varying degrees of disclosure are a consequence of legal, competitive, and societal pressures. In the case of Switzerland, secrecy is one of its greatest natural treasures: it is a major reason why many individuals and companies place their money there, or are incorporated or do business there. If full disclosure were required, much of the foreign funds, and many foreign business activities, would be withdrawn, thus reducing employment, income, and taxes in Switzerland. Needless to say, then, the Swiss government does not require, or push for much public disclosure by firms or individuals. And besides, the government already has access to the financial statements of Swiss enterprises. At the same time, Swiss banks are the largest investors in Swiss firms, and due to their creditor/owner relationships with Swiss firms, they also have ready access to company financial statements. Finally, many Swiss firms are family-owned, private companies. For all of these reasons, the public disclosure of financial information is neither needed nor extensively practiced.

In Scandinavia, by contrast, many of the large firms are government owned (partially or wholly), and the nation's economics is characterized by political socialism. Although the government has its own direct access to the financial information of companies, its role as social steward requires it to have companies provide financial information to the society directly via highly disclosed corporate financial reports. In the United States, on the other hand, the relatively extensive disclosure requirements have different reasons. The United States has a large, highly educated investing public, and a large number of publicly owned firms. The U.S. also had, when corporate disclosure practices were less than considerable, a few historic financial scandals and a few dramatic collapses of business enterprises. Therefore, over time there have been major increases in the requirements for corporate disclosure in the United States.

The social, legal, and political conditions of other countries differ to some degree from each other and from the three countries just mentioned. Therefore, the degree of public disclosure required throughout the world varies accordingly. Still, the need to obtain funds from the world's investing public often forces firms to increase their level of disclosure, no matter what the local laws, business practices, or social desires may be. As the world's economy becomes increasingly competitive, more and more firms find it necessary to tap international investors for the funds needed for successful competition. These sophisticated investors want information about the firms that want to use their money. Thus has the general level of corporate disclosure increased.

Note, though, that disclosure takes many forms. In some cases, it includes detailed data; in others, it is only explanations of data. To these nuances and specific aspects of disclosure we now turn.

Detailed and Explanatory Notes

Financial reports are always summaries, and thus, by definition, leave out certain details. The question is, how much is left out? At one extreme there is the narrative statement that says simply and only that profits increased over last year's. Greater disclosure would say, in quantitative or percentage terms, how much profits increased. More disclosure would show the specific numbers, for example, profits in 19X1 were $2 million, and in 19X2 were $2.5 million. Still more disclosure would show how the profit figures were generated, for example, what the total revenues and total expenses were—then even a detailed breakdown of those revenues and expenses could be disclosed, and so on. Thus, how much information is provided is a key aspect of disclosure.

For an MNE, the reporting of details is more complex because it has so many more details to report. In addition, many of those details require considerably more explanation, because typical users may not be familiar with the events in or accounting procedures of other countries, or with the accounting procedures required for consolidating foreign operations. Therefore, there is a greater need both for detail and for explanations in the financial reports of MNEs. At the same time, our earlier discussions should have made it clear that providing such information is not an easy task. In addition, sometimes summarizing everything into one consolidated report hinders rather than helps the users of financial information. Thus, segment reporting has been devised as a means of untangling the complexities of an MNE's operations.

Segment Reporting

One should not be misled: there is a great deal to be said in favor of consolidating or otherwise aggregating the financial statements of interrelated accounting entities which partly form a larger economic unit such as an MNE. This has been the traditional practice in the U.S. and the U.K. because stockholders, potential investors, creditors, and other users of financial statements are interested in the financial position and the results of operations of the firm as a whole. But given the vast complexity and diversity of the activities of major corporations, consolidated statements can befuddle or otherwise confuse even intelligent readers.

To help the users of financial statements more clearly evaluate the performance of a firm, smaller segments of the firm should be represented in financial reports. Such segmentation can be by industry, by product line, or by geographic location. The increasing sophistication of users, combined with increasing demands for disaggregated information by several government agencies, today makes segment reporting a necessity for large firms in general, and for MNEs in particular. Thus, an important issue at present is how segments should be determined, since segmentation relates to the full disclosure concept.

In general, a segment can be a profit center, a product line, a division, a geographic area, or a customer group. Therefore, in dealing with segmentation, one must judge how to group the different activities of a major corporation. For example, FASB in its Statement No. 14 defines a geographic segment for a multinational as those "individual countries or groups of countries as may be determined to be appropriate in an enterprise's particular circumstances."[14] This definition allows for a great deal of latitude when management decides on segmentation.

However, corporations are not entirely at liberty in their segment reporting. FASB *requires* the identification of four types of business segments: industry lines, foreign operations, export sales, and major customers. The determining factor for reporting segments (not to exceed ten in number) is a 10% rule: 10% or more of worldwide total revenues, of total operating profit or loss (deleted for foreign operations), or of total assets. For example, even though a firm may sell over a thousand different products, perhaps only fifty are exported. If the combined export sales of these fifty products exceeds 10% of total corporate sales, then the firm can and must report these export sales as a separate segment in its financial reports. Or, if the thousand products can be grouped into four categories, such as synthetic fibers, agricultural chemicals, chemical intermediates, and industrial chemicals, the 10% rule must be applied to each group to determine whether any one of the four groups must be reported separately in the firm's financial statements. For example, if the four groups represent 9%, 7%, 3%, and 81%, respectively, of the firm's total sales, then a separate disclosure

[14]Financial Accounting Standards Board, *Financial Reporting for Segments of a Business Enterprise*, Statement No. 14 (Stamford, Connecticut: FASB, December 1976).

(a segmentation) must be made for the fourth group, but not for the other three groups.

The same procedure applies if the 10% rule fits a particular geographic area or group of countries (such as South America or Europe) or a group of customers (such as the government or retail stores). In addition, the combined sales to unaffiliated customers in reportable segments should be at least 75% of the total worldwide sales to unaffiliated customers. To maintain harmony in financial reporting, the U.S. Securities and Exchange Commission (SEC) decided to make its lines-of-business reporting rules conform to the segment reporting guidelines of FASB.[15]

Other organizations, such as the European Economic Community (EEC) in its Fourth Directive, the Organization for Economic Cooperation and Development (OECD), the United Nations Center on Transnational Corporations (UNCTC), and the International Accounting Standards Committee (IASC) in its Definitive Standard No. 14, have dealt with segment reporting, but generally without specifying the precise criteria for segmentation, such as the 10% and 75% tests of FASB.[16] In general, these organizations in addition require the disclosure of sales and other operating revenues by industry lines and by geographical areas. For example, the EEC has proposed that firms based outside the community which have operations inside the community prepare and disclose a segmented report about their combined European operations. Thus General Motors, for example, because of its operations in Europe, would have to prepare a special segmented "European Community" report, even though it might not have to do so for U.S. reporting purposes.

One of the major needs for segmentation concerns the users of finan-

---

[15]Securities and Exchange Commission, "Industry Segment Reporting: Adoption of Disclosure Regulation and Amendments of Disclosure Forms and Rules," *Accounting Series Release No. 236* (Washington, D.C.: SEC, December 1977) and also "Industry Segment Determination," *Accounting Series Release No. 244* (Washington, D.C.: SEC, March 1978).

[16]European Economic Community, "Principles of Accounting and Disclosures," *Fourth Directive* (July 25, 1978); Organization for Economic Cooperation and Development, "International Investment and Multinational Enterprises" (Paris: OECD, 1979); United Nations Commission on Transnational Corporations, "International Standards of Accounting and Reporting" (New York: UNCTC, 1977); and International Accounting Standards Committee, "Reporting Financial Information by Segment," *Definitive Standard No. 14* (London: IASC, August 1981).

cial reports being able to identify corporate dependencies: how dependent a firm is on a particular customer, geographic area, or product line. The greater the dependency, the higher the risk the company faces, since if something unfavorable happens to that customer, geographic area, or product, a significant portion of the firm's revenues may disappear. Naturally, the higher the risk a company faces, the higher the risk the investor or creditor faces. Therefore, investors and creditors want to have a good understanding of the potential risks the company faces—an understanding that segment reporting can provide.

For example, consider two large U.S.-based oil companies: one has most of its oil wells in the Middle East, and is not diversified into other businesses; the other has most of its wells in the United States, and is diversified into coal and the construction business. On a geographic basis, the first company is highly dependent on a very politically unstable (that is, a risky) geographic area; the second firm is also dependent on one geographic area, but at a relatively low risk. But what is more, if instability in the Middle East causes the first firm's flow of oil to be interrupted, or stopped permanently, it has few other sources of oil, and no other businesses to cushion the shock. The second oil company, however, could absorb some of the financial shock either by expanding its U.S. production or by relying on its other businesses. A risk-adverse investor or creditor therefore would probably choose the second company over the first; but without segment reporting, he might not know of any differences in risk and mistakenly choose the first company.

Among the world's companies, segment reporting is practiced extensively by Scandinavian and British MNEs, to a somewhat lesser extent by U.S. MNEs, to a far lesser extent by continental European MNEs, and hardly at all by the MNEs of most other countries.

Yet, while segment reporting benefits the users of financial information, it has certain drawbacks for the companies themselves. For example, segment reporting provides information about the firm's activities that may be useful to competitors, information that competitors might not be able to obtain from any other source. Segment reporting may also adversely influence a firm's ability to raise capital. Finally, it may provide information to governments that the firm would prefer to conceal.

That is to say, segment reporting is more disclosure than most firms care to make. Thus, unless a firm is constrained by legal, competitive, or social pressures to do so, it will probably resist segment reporting. And even when it is forced into segment reporting by law, it may deliberately portray its segments in a manner that limits their usefulness to the users of financial information. For example, it may report the geographic segment, "Europe and the Middle East," or "Canada and Central America." These geographic segments, being so large and diverse (both politically and economically), provide little enlightening information to users. As we mentioned earlier, the existing rules for determining what constitutes a segment allow firms considerable flexibility; thus, segment reporting in reality is often less useful than in theory. Still, perhaps some segment reporting is better than none.

That "some is better than none" may (or may not) apply generally to several other aspects of corporate disclosure—aspects to which we now turn.

Financial Forecasts

Another controversial issue surrounding disclosure is this: Should firms include financial forecasts in their annual reports? Such information is available internally in most firms, but seldom is it made public. Many researchers and practitioners have shown that such forecasts have reliability problems, among others.[17] But whatever the problems related to the inclusion of forecasts in annual reports, the problems are even greater for MNEs—for the simple reason that MNEs operate in many countries. MNEs would have to forecast the conditions of and operational results in many different economic and political environments. Think also on the etiquette involved. Firms making public their forecasts of the economic and political conditions of foreign countries could anger or embarrass those foreign governments, and the government of the parent company as well. A financial forecast could be potentially useful for private investors or creditors, but the negative reactions of even one government could cause problems for the unwary MNE. An unfavorable forecast could also prompt competitors to take actions ultimately injurious to the MNE. Neither result of publishing the forecast would be in the best interests of the firm, or its investors

[17]For example see: B. Basi, K. Carey and R. Turark, "A Comparison of the Accuracy of Corporate and Securities Analysts Forecasts of Earnings," *Accounting Review*, April 1976, pp. 244–254; Financial Executives Institute, "How Accurate are Forecasts?" *Financial Executive* March 1973; B. Jaggi, "Further Evidence of the Accuracy of Management Forecasts *vis a vis* Analyst's Forecasts," *Accounting Review*, January 1980, pp. 96–107.

and creditors. Thus, the disclosure of corporate forecasts is seldom practiced unless required by law.[18]

Special "Impact" Reports

People generally think of financial reports in terms of income statements and balance sheets, and occasionally in terms of flow-of-funds reports. However, financial reporting in many countries includes more than just these three typical varieties. For reasons surrounding currency control and the balance of payments, for example, some countries require firms to prepare special reports on the impact of their international transactions.

In the Philippines and Indonesia—to name just two countries—how much foreign currency an investment will generate or use up is the government's major consideration when it decides to approve or veto an investment proposal. Some developing countries go even further by requesting or requiring firms to report on the total economic impact they have on the country—that is, a firm must show, in specific terms, how much the nation's economy is improved (or injured) as a result of the firm's investments and operations. These reports involve estimating both direct and indirect (or multiplier) economic effects.[19] And in an ever increasing number of countries, including most nations in Europe, firms are required by law to report information about some aspects of the firm's "social impact." These "social reports" are meant to assess, for example, whether a firm's employees are happier, safer, more secure, and more skilled; or how the firm has affected the general welfare of the society by increasing or decreasing pollution, for instance.

These social reports go by various names in different countries: "bilan social" (social balance sheet) in France, "social jaarreslag" in the Netherlands, "social bilanz" in Germany. In each country, they have a somewhat different focus, depending on the major concerns of each nation's society. Whatever their focus though, two things are clear. First, social reports are increasingly demanded worldwide; and second, they pose several new and unique problems for accountants who must

[18]For a comprehensive treatment of forecast disclosure practices in Europe, see S. J. Gray, "Managerial Forecasts in European MNC Reporting," *Journal of International Business Studies*, Fall 1978, pp. 21–32.

[19]Examples of indirect effects are the number of jobs created or eliminated in other businesses in the economy as a result of the firm's activity, and the resultant effects on income, taxes, and so on.

prepare them. As for the latter situation, accountants in most countries are not sufficiently trained to prepare social reports adequately. In fact, some argue that no one is sufficiently trained to do so because many social reports require estimations that cannot be made in a reliable, verifiable, or unbiased way.

For example, how can anyone quantify the exact impact upon society of a firm's $1 million expenditure on pollution abatement equipment? True, one can measure the direct input cost ($1 million), and the quantitative reduction of pollution in terms of "particles emitted." But how can one say, in quantitative terms, exactly how much the society is improved as a result of the expenditure? Would the society have been even better off if the firm had used the $1 million to expand production and as a result hire 100 previously unemployed people instead?

What is more, a social impact considered desirable in some countries may be considered undesirable in other countries. A program that would increase the number of black managers in a firm might be well received in the U.S., but ill received in South Africa. Whose judgment should govern the MNE?

From an accountant's perspective, these problems and others related to social impact accounting, as well as the problems associated with preparing reports that are not income statements or balance sheets, can be a quandry at best, and a nightmare at worst. Fortunately, such reports lack specific accounting standards and procedures for their preparation, which gives accountants some flexibility and leeway. Many of these reports can be nonquantitative narratives; when they are quantitative, often they are limited to input measures (that is, direct expenditures). And in most cases where output measures are required, they tend to be easily verifiable—for example, the quantity of pollution reduced, the number of accidents decreased, and so forth. But the growing socialism and social consciousness throughout the world will certainly increase the number and complexity of social reports and other "impact" reports that multinational firms will have to supply. Therefore, accountants must be prepared.

The Mechanics of Report Preparation

For a multinational enterprise operating in a dozen countries, the sheer volume and diversity of the reports it must prepare annually is awesome. So too are the mechanics of preparing these reports. Typically, several reports must be prepared for each country, often several consolidated reports for its home country, and segmented reports for various groups—all according to different accounting procedures, and all on different schedules. Here is just a simple example. By Colombian law, all firms must keep records and prepare reports on the basis of the *calendar* year—from January 1 to December 31. If a U.S. parent firm with a Colombian subsidiary uses a fiscal year different from the calendar year, say, from June 1 to May 31, it still must close its subsidiary's books on December 31 for Colombian reporting purposes, even though it will not close its own books and its consolidated books until May 31. Imagine the reporting problems that could cause. Imagine what the firm would face with subsidiaries in twelve countries, each with a different fiscal year.

Preparing and transmitting accounting reports from a dozen countries in a correct and timely manner, then, is no easy task. It requires a large number of trained personnel, a sophisticated internal information and reporting system, time, patience, and money. These accounting complexities will be discussed in greater detail in the following chapter.

SUMMARY

Financial reporting for a multinational firm is far more complicated than accounting for a purely domestic firm. The two most important difficulties facing MNEs are operating in different currencies and in different accounting systems. MNEs also must produce a number and variety of reports much greater than domestic firms do. In sum, then, international financial reporting requires considerable expertise to comprehend and to practice.

STUDY QUESTIONS FOR CHAPTER 5

1. If an MNE had domestic sales of $12 million, sales in Japan of 25 million yen, and sales in Brazil of 10 million cruzeiros, what was the value of its consolidated sales if the exchange rates were $1.00 = 250 yen and $1.00 = 50 cruzeiros?
2. Suppose in the following year the same sales were achieved in each country (in local currency), but the dollar had strengthened against the cruziero and weakened against the yen, each by 10%. Would

the MNE's consolidated sales (in dollar terms) be higher or lower than in Question 1, and if so, by how much?

3. Explain the essential difference between a transaction gain or loss and a translation gain or loss.
4. What do you see as the advantages and disadvantages of the one-transaction perspective versus the two-transaction perspective in treating transaction gains and losses?
5. How can a firm eliminate the risks of transaction losses due to changes in exchange rates?
6. How can a firm eliminate the risks of translation losses due to changes in exchange rates?
7. Discuss the major differences in the currency translation procedures of balance sheet accounts under the current–noncurrent, monetary–nonmonetary, temporal, and current rate methods.
8. Discuss the changes in reporting foreign exhcnage gains and losses occasioned by FAS #52. (Compare it to FAS #8.)
9. Other than exchange rate conversion problems, what are the additional problems in preparing consolidated financial statements?
10. Why would firms prefer *not* to make a full disclosure? What environmental conditions cause (or force) them to disclose more information?
11. From the viewpoint of a user, why are segmented reports desirable? From an issuer's viewpoint, why are segmented reports undesirable?
12. From the viewpont of a user, why is the inclusion of financial forecasts desirable? From an issuer's viewpoint, why is their inclusion undesirable?
13. What are some of the major problems accountants face in preparing "social reports"?
14. Why do MNEs typically have more sets of books than domestic firms?

ADDITIONAL REFERENCES

1. AlHashim, Dhia D. and Robertson, James W. *Accounting for Multinational Enterprises.* Indianapolis, Indiana: Bobbs-Merrill Educational Publishing, 1978, Chapter 4.
2. AlHashim, Dhia D. and Robertson, James W. *Contemporary Issues in Accounting.* Indianapolis, Indiana: Bobbs-Merrill Educational Publishing, 1979, Chapter 4.

3. Aliber, R. Z. and Stickney, C. P. "Measures of Foreign Exchange Exposure." *Accounting Review*, January 1975.
4. Arpan, Jeffrey S. and Radebaugh, Lee H. *International Accounting and Multinational Enterprises.* Boston, Massachusetts: Warren, Gorham & Lamont, 1981.
5. Choi, Frederick D. S. and Mueller, Gerhard G. *An Introduction to Multinational Accounting.* Englewood Cliffs, New Jersey: Prentice-Hall, 1978.
6. Dufey, G. "Corporate Finance and Exchange Rate Variations." *Financial Management*, Summer 1972.
7. Financial Accounting Standards Board, *Statement of Financial Accounting Standards No. 14, Financial Reporting for Segments of a Business Enterprise.* Stamford, Conn.: FASB, 1976.
8. Gray, S. J. "Segment Reporting and the EEC Multinationals." *Journal of Accounting Research*, Autumn 1978, pp. 242–253.
9. Hussey, Roger. "Who Reads Employee Reports?" St. Edmund Hall, England: Touche Ross, October 1979.
10. International Accounting Standards Committee. *Financial Statements.* London: IASC, 1977.
11. International Accounting Standards Committee. *International Accounting Standard 1, Disclosure of Accounting Policies.* London: IASC, 1975.
12. International Accounting Standards Committee. *International Accounting Standard 5, Information to Be Disclosed in International Accounting Standards Committee (IASC). International Accounting Standard 3, Consolidated Financial Statements.* London: IASC, 1976.
13. Kramer, Gerald. "Small Companies Rush for Aid in Handling Foreign Currency Dealings." *Business Week*, 6 December 1976.
14. Linowes, David F. "The Accounting Profession and Social Progress." *Journal of Accountancy*, July 1973, pp. 32–40.
15. Nobes, Christopher. "A Review of the Translation Debate." *Accounting and Business Research*, Autumn 1980.
16. Parker, R. H. "Explaining National Differences in Consolidated Accounts." *Accounting and Business Research*, Summer 1977, pp. 203–207.
17. Parkinson, R. MacDonald, *Translation of Foreign Currencies.* Toronto: Canadian Institute of Chartered Accountants, 1972.
18. Rosenfield, Paul. "General Price-Level Accounting and Foreign Operations." *Journal of Accountancy*, February 1971.

19. Shank, John K. "FASB Statement No. 8 Resolved Foreign Currency Accounting, Or Did It?" *Financial Analysts Journal*, July–August 1976.

20. Shoenfeld, Hanns-Martin. *The Status of Social Reporting in Selected Countries.* Urbana, Ill.: Center for International Education and Research in Accounting, 1978.

21. Smith, A. F. "Temporal Method: Temporal Mode." *Management Accounting*, February 1978.

22. Swoboda, Peter. "Comparison of Consolidated Financial Statements in the United States and West Germany." *International Journal of Accounting*, Spring, 1966, pp. 9–24.

23. Task Force on Corporate Social Performance. *Corporate Social Reporting in the United States and Western Europe.* Washington, D.C.: Department of Commerce, July 1979.

24. Walker, D. P. *An Economic Analysis of Foreign Exchange Risk.* (Research Committee Occasional Paper No. 14.) London: ICAEW, 1978.

Chapter 6

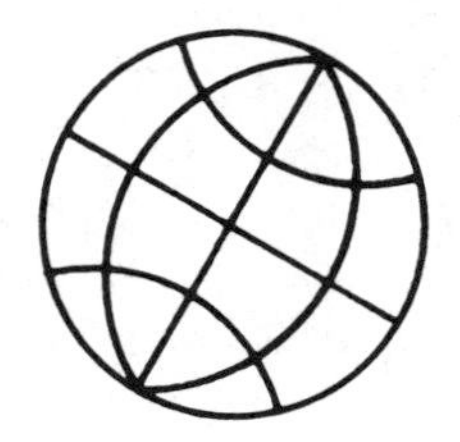

Managerial Accounting Complexities in International Business

Essentially, managerial (or internal) accounting provides economic information useful for managers making decisions, specifically, decisions about how to plan, direct, and control an organization's operations. The amount of information required to make these decisions properly is considerable, even for small proprietorships. For large MNEs, the amount of information is staggering. Hence, MNEs use incredible international information systems to collect, store, and direct information to the right people at the right time. The process of monitoring and evaluating what actually occurs in the firm's operations is awesome.

This chapter will provide some examples of how operating internationally complicates the already problematic business of managerial accounting for a purely domestic organization. The four main areas of planning, costing, controlling, and organizing will be examined.

PLANNING

Planning concerns the operations of the firm in the future: What must it do to survive and grow? For most companies, this question is asked only in a domestic context. That is, U.S. domestic firms, for example, think about expanding their capacity only in the United States, or they think about increasing their sales only in the U.S. market, and so on. However, for an increasing number of firms, and especially for MNEs, these questions must be considered in an international context: Should sales be increased at home or abroad? Where is the best place in the world to expand capacity?

The basic decision tools and the general types of information needed to make planning decisions are essentially the same whether the decision is domestically or internationally focussed. However, the *applicability* of some of the decision tools is often impaired primarily because the information needed for international decisions is often lacking.

The Planning Process

Because someone has yet to develop a foolproof method for forecasting the future, planning is a difficult task and an imprecise process. Three things, however, are clear in the realm of international accounting: some planning is better than no planning; some planning methods are better than others; and planning is more difficult for an MNE.[1]

Some planning is better than no planning because there are benefits from the planning process itself. It forces management to think about their operations and about their company's position. The more comprehensive and detailed the planning process, the more management must move from broad generalities to specific, measurable objectives. Uncertainties can be translated into risks, and the degree of risk can be reduced.

Some planning processes are better than others. In general, the more

---

[1]For a good overview of the planning problems of MNEs, see William L. Cain, "International Planning: Mission Impossible?," *Columbia Journal of World Business*, July/August, 1970, pp. 58ff.

reliable the information that can be gathered, and the more accurate the assessment of this information, the better the plan will be.

The complexities of planning for international operations stem from the greater uncertainties, both economic and political, that MNEs face. Forecasts of economic and competitive conditions in at least two countries must be made, along with forecasts of any likely political actions. These forecasts require information. However, the information that is relatively easy to obtain in one country is not always easily obtained or even available in another. In addition, a person in one country may have difficulty properly analyzing information obtained from and about another country, because no one understands another country as well as he understands his own. A native Brazilian can understand, analyze, and predict the economic and political conditions of Brazil better than a native New Yorker can.

Note, too, that economic, political, and social conditions are more stable in some countries than in others, and hence they are easier to analyze and predict. Oddly enough, while planning a company's operations for the highly unstable environments in which it may operate is clearly difficult to do, it is yet perhaps even more important than the planning for stable environments.

For example, planning a company's operations in a country with an inflation rate of over 100% per year is extremely difficult, because it is difficult to predict what materials and labor will cost, how much the firm's products can be sold for, and so on. At the same time, *not* planning in this hyperinflationary environment is even more risky than not planning in a stable environment, because the firm's capital can be eroded more quickly, or sufficient funds will not be available to purchase the increasingly expensive inputs to production. A firm operating in several countries therefore must make specific plans for each country, taking into account each nation's unique conditions.

In addition, if a subsidiary in one country ships to an affiliated firm in another country finished products or components for subsequent sale or assembly, the parent firm must anticipate how changes in the environment of the supplying country will affect transfers to the other country, and vice versa. For example, a balance of payments problem in the buying subsidiary's country could result in bans or restrictions on imports—including those imports from the subsidiary's affiliate in the other country. Or a balance of payments problem could cause the importing country to raise tariffs on imported merchandise, thus increasing purchase prices for the buying subsidiary. Similar increases in the purchasing costs of the buying subsidiary could occur if the country of the supplying subsidiary had such a large *surplus* in its balance of payments that the exchange value of its currency went up. Thus, for example, a quantity that used to cost $10,000 might now cost the buying subsidiary $12,000.

Other difficulties in the planning process concern cultural differences. People in some countries are fatalistic, believing that what happens in life—and in business—is beyond any mortal's control. Under these cultural conditions, planning is often considered irrelevant and futile, because planning assumes that the future can be altered by taking certain actions in the present. When some multinational firms ask the managers of their foreign subsidiaries to plan, they often encounter resistance. Some of their managers, because of certain cultural influences, are basically fatalistic. In addition, the reluctance of foreign subsidiary managers to contribute to the planning process can be the result of a cultural inferiority complex. That is, some foreign managers believe that the corporate headquarter's staff is, by definition, wiser and more knowledgeable than they are themselves. How, they ask, could they possibly improve on headquarter's plans?[2] Whatever the reasons subsidiary managers have for not participating in the planning process, the planning process suffers because important data and perspectives from those "on the scene" are lost.

Finally, some foreign subsidiary managers feel that the headquarter's staff does not fully understand or appreciate the situation in the subsidiary's country or market. The foreign managers also may be unaware of larger global objectives and considerations that headquarters is accounting for in the development of its plans. Either situation can add frustration and time to the planning process, or prevent the planning process from being completed effectively.

Thus, the entire question of participation in planning must be approached carefully.[3] Naturally, both headquarters and subsidiaries should be involved in the planning process. Without the involvement of headquarters, the MNE's operations can fall apart quickly, and a major competitive advantage of being an MNE may be lost: the ability

[2]This type of individual is often referred to as a xenophile.

[3]For a more detailed discussion of management personality styles and perspectives, and how they affect planning and operations of an MNE, see Howard Perlmutter, "The Tortuous Evolution of A Multinational Corporation," *Columbia Journal of World Business*, January/February 1969. pp. 19–33.

to coordinate operations on a global scale. At the same time, subsidiary participation in planning is essential to make sure that plans are in fact feasible, and to better insure that subsidiary managers will carry out the plans decided upon.

To understand better some of the complexities of international planning, let us examine a few specific areas of managerial accounting covered by the planning process.

Capital Budgeting: Investments

Capital budgeting includes the process of planning and evaluating long-term investment proposals. A firm often must decide whether to invest in a proposed project, whether to keep or replace existing equipment, and whether to keep or divest existing plants or operations.

The major difficulty in making any of these decisions concerns the uncertainty of the future. That is, the decision maker cannot accurately predict what the future competitive conditions will be—for example, what future sales revenues or production costs might be. In some cases, the actual cost of the proposed investment itself may not be known because the future is so uncertain. For example, the building of a plant may happen several years after the time when it was planned, during which time the costs of labor, material, and land may rise or fall.

To help solve this dilemma, a number of analytical techniques have been developed, such as payback, discounted cash flow, net present value, and internal rate of return. Each seeks to estimate and quantify the future expenses and revenues surrounding a particular business proposal, and all except the payback method put these amounts into current dollar values. While there are many problems involved in determining such estimates just for a domestic decision, the difficulties are even greater for an international decision. For example, changes in exchange rates may alter future revenue and expense flows which were calculated in dollars at the current exchange rate. Thus, a proposed plant in Germany at a cost of 20 million DM has a U.S. dollar cost of \$10 million if the exchange rate is \$1 = 2DM. But if the DM strengthens relative to the dollar making the dollar equal to only 1.5 DM, the dollar cost of the plant increases to \$13.33 million (20 million DM ÷ 1.5 = \$13.33 million). These same kinds of effects occur with future revenue flows. If the DM strengthens, translated dollar revenues increase; if it weakens, translated dollar revenues decline.

In addition to varying exchange rates, there are other problems to consider. First, the foreign country probably has a different inflation rate. Second, there is a chance that the foreign government may restrict the amount of money that can be taken out of the country and sent back to the parent. Third, the government may decide to take over (or nationalize) the foreign venture.[4] Each of these would affect the estimated dollar value of future revenues. Finally, competitive conditions in the foreign country will usually vary and so require additional estimations of changes in foreign market conditions, competitors, and their impact on future expense and revenue flows.

All these factors make it more difficult to use the decision-making tools used so widely in domestic situations. These factors also require that more information be collected and analyzed. Hence, there's more work for the MNE's accountants. In sum, capital budgeting becomes more complicated, less precise, and more difficult in an international context. This is not to say that it should not or cannot be done. It can and must be done, but greater caution must be used by an MNE in interpreting the results of capital budgeting techniques.

Budgeting for Operations

Another important facet of planning is the operations budgeting process: deciding how to allocate scarce financial resources among the competing needs of operating units. Budgeting is not only an integral part of the planning process, but an essential part of the control process, as well—budgeting controls the generation and deployment of funds and so controls the activities of the firm.

As far as the planning aspects of budgeting are concerned, estimates must be made of both financial needs and the potential sources of funds. The needs are based on the specific objectives of the parent, each affiliate, and the company as a whole. That is, budgeting attempts to estimate what it will cost to accomplish each objective. The potential sources of funds are determined by adding up the available beginning funds, funds expected to be generated by planned operations, and outside or externally obtainable funds. The last of these three sources becomes important when the first two are estimated as insufficient in their amount or badly timed for the estimated needs. The entire budgeting

---

[4]In a nationalization, the government assumes ownership of a firm, often paying little or no compensation to the previous owners.

process for an MNE hardly differs in its structure from the budgeting process a domestic company uses. Differences do emerge out of the complexities and many options an MNE faces. The complexities arise on several fronts.

First, as noted above, changes in exchange rates affect the flows of funds. A parent budgets $1 million of its funds for its French subsidiary because it has been determined that the French operation will need 4 million french francs (ff) in the coming year. The $1 million amount is budgeted based on the exchange rate being $1 = 4 ff. Thus the budget is set, and a loan is prepared. Then the French franc increases in value so that $1 = 2.5 ff. When the loan goes through and the dollars are converted, the French subsidiary only gets ff 2.5 million—an amount insufficient to cover its needs. Thus, it may have to reduce its operations or borrow an additional ff 1.5 million at higher short-term interest rates to cover its needs. As you can see, then, budgeting must try to take into account any potential changes in the exchange rates for the currencies in which foreign subsidiaries operate.

Second, changes in the competitive or environmental conditions of one country may affect the flow of funds from the operations of a subsidiary in that country to a subsidiary in another country. For example, an MNE plans that a Peruvian affiliate will generate funds to be used by a French affiliate. But when the time comes to transfer the funds certain balance of payments problems in Peru cause its government to stop all outward flows of corporate funds. The French subsidiary is then faced with the same problem as in the previous example: insufficient funds.

Third, even determining the true (that is, the effective) interest rate for budgeting and planning purposes is not always easy.[5] An MNE wants to borrow money at the cheapest rate, but what the cheapest rate is will depend not just on the nominal rates but also on differential inflation rates and exchange rate changes. For example, it may appear to be better for a French affiliate to borrow funds from a German bank at 10% rather than from a Mexican bank at 30%. Yet, if the French franc weakens against the deutschmark it will take more francs to repay the German loan, thereby increasing the effective interest rate. On the other hand, should the franc strengthen against the peso, it will take

[5]For a detailed discussion of effective interest rates, see R. Rodriguez and E. Carter, *International Financial Management*, 2d ed. (Englewood Cliffs, N.J.: Prentice-Hall, 1979) pp. 221–225, and 246–247.

fewer francs to repay the Mexican loan, thereby lowering the effective interest rate. Therefore, it is conceivable that the effective interest rate for borrowing from Mexico may be lower than borrowing from Germany, even though the nominal German rate is one third the Mexican rate.

Budgeting for international operations, then, must anticipate many more factors and uncertainties than budgeting for domestic operations. Like the planning process itself, an MNE's budgeting must include many more contingency plans than a domestic firm would have to provide for unexpected or inaccurately estimated changes in the conditions under which the firm operates.

COSTING

Product Costing

With few exceptions, product cost accounting concepts are universally applicable. That is, cost accumulation systems (such as job-order costing, and process costing), cost concepts (full cost, direct cost, and so on), and cost analyses (incremental and C/V/P models) are just as applicable to MNEs as to domestic firms. However, MNEs face tricky complications.

First of all, if a product is made in one country and shipped to an affiliate in a second country, changes in the exchange rates will affect product costing. The same is true if the manufacturing unit in the first country uses imported raw materials or semifinished goods. And if it both imports material and, after adding value to or completing the product, ships that product to a third country (or back to the original supply country), two exchange rate fluctuations and possibly three currencies must be considered. Tariffs and other forms of customs duties also must be added to product costs, and occasionally export taxes as well. Also, adding to product costs are international transportation and insurance fees, and other expenses related to obtaining government approval, such as the fees for applying for foreign exchange to import the product. On the other hand, any export subsidies (such as tax credits or rebates for exporting) should be *subtracted* from the product cost.

With all of these complexities to consider, one might wonder why any firm would bother with multicountry shipments. But the answer is fairly simple. Some countries have low production costs for certain products, but are not the best (that is, are not the most profitable) countries for sales. From an MNE's point of view, it makes economic sense to produce each part of a product in the cheapest place, assemble it in the cheapest place, and ultimately sell it in the most profitable place (or where the market is best). This is called international production rationalization, a concept which underlies Ford Motor company's "World Car," for example. Axles for the car are manufactured in one country, engines in a second country, transmissions in a third country, and other parts in other countries—all for assembly in one or two other countries for ultimate sale around the world.

You can imagine the significant problems facing the poor cost accountant who must estimate what making the final car will cost next year, or even worse, two or three years hence (for long-range planning purposes). Any cost estimate must consider numerous inflation rates, potential changes in the exchange rates, changes in plant utilization and worker productivity, changes in tariffs, taxes, and subsidies in a number of different countries, and changes in international transportation and insurance rates, as well. Yet the magnitude and complexity of the task does not dissuade companies from being MNEs. The rewards of international production rationalization can be substantial and well worth the additional managerial accounting and other costs.

Accountants trying to develop a worldwide "standard cost" for a product produced in several countries face similar problems, even if no international shipping takes place. The production process in a country with inexpensive labor may be *labor* intensive, but the process may be *capital* intensive in a country with higher labor costs. In no two countries are inflation or worker productivity rates the same, which complicates matters even further. MNEs also encounter the unavailability of data and the inadequate cost accounting skills of professionals in many countries. These latter problems can make product costing even in only one foreign country a difficult task.

Finally, there is the question of the international allocation of costs. What if costs are incurred in one country, but affiliates in other countries benefit from those costs? Research and development expenses and numerous types of headquarters expenses are a few examples of such costs. If the parent provides marketing services in its own country, incurring marketing expenses for a product that it produces in another country, should the producing affiliate's product cost include an allocation of the parent company's marketing expenses? And if so, how and how much? Similarly, if the parent firm's R & D lab spends $5 million on developing a new manufacturing process, should the foreign affiliates absorb some of this $5 million expense? These questions concern *internal* transfers and their pricing—usually referred to as transfer pricing, or intercorporate pricing. It represents not only a complex area of costing, but one of the most controversial areas of international business. Thus, we might benefit from examining transfer pricing in more detail.

Transfer Pricing

The marketing and R & D expense allocation examples above are only two of the many opportunities for transfer pricing within an MNE. Consider also the pricing of goods shipped among units of an MNE (raw materials, semifinished and finished goods); fees for patents, trademarks, and licenses granted to affiliates; the interest on internal loans; the expenses of management consulting and training programs done for the benefit of affiliates; and general headquarters' overhead, to name just a few other areas where expense allocation becomes an issue.

Certainly a logical argument can be made for allocating such expenses to affiliates—either as part of their product cost or as a general expense to their profit and loss statement. After all, if affiliates benefit from expenditures made by other parts of the MNE, why shouldn't they bear some of the expense? But what if they do *not* benefit from the expense? For example, what if our hypothetical $5 million R & D project does not result in anything useful at all, or if it does, what if the benefit is not received directly by the affiliate (a new manufacturing process, for example, does not benefit the affiliate directly when the affiliate is a sales office and not a manufacturing unit)? In such cases, MNEs typically argue that expense allocations are still justified on the grounds that all affiliates are part of a global family, and therefore should share in the risks, expenses, and benefits of that global family and its activities.

Still, we must pause to consider a more basic question you may be wondering about—namely, who cares? If it's all internal, why should anyone care whether costs are allocated or not? After all, if it *is* one big family then the total expenses are the sum of all unit expenses, no matter who incurs or absorbs them.

Therefore, it shouldn't make any difference if expenses are allocated or not, right? Wrong. It *does* make a difference.[6] First of all, if individual units are treated as profit centers, transfer pricing affects their profitability. Thus, a Brazilian manager does not want his or her costs increased (and profits decreased) artificially by a cost allocation from the New York headquarters. Second, and more important, allocating expenses to foreign affiliates lowers their taxable income and so lowers the tax revenues of the foreign subsidiary's country. This can be impolitic. The leaders and tax officials of these countries obviously are not likely to favor such allocation practices. In addition, if and when the affiliate actually pays for the internal transfers and the allocated expenses, its country's balance of payments is affected adversely as money leaves the country—something that is also viewed unfavorably by the nation's politicians. Thus, there are both internal and external relations problems generated by international transfer pricing. While most of the internal problems can be solved by the MNE using an appropriate performance evaluation system (as discussed later in this chapter), the external problems are not so easily solved, particularly when there is no clearly identifiable benefit to the subsidiary being charged.

That the firm in their country is part of a large MNE tends not to impress local government officials. They only tend to notice that less taxes are collected and more money leaves the country as expenses are charged to the MNE's subsidiary. They are also concerned because they know that historically many MNEs have used transfer pricing to thwart or circumvent government policy.[7] For example, some countries limit or even temporarily ban dividend payments from subsidiaries in their countries to foreign-based parent companies. Yet MNEs can evade the limitation or ban by raising transfer prices on goods shipped to, and/or services provided for, the foreign subsidiaries; and in some cases, they even bill subsidiaries for totally ficticious expenses. These practices have led some countries, such as Brazil, to prohibit *any* intercorporate payments for anything other than products, and to carefully scrutinize all transfer pricing on products, as well.

---

[6]For more detailed discussion of what difference transfer pricing can make to an MNE, see J. Shulman, *Transfer Pricing in Multinational Business* (Harvard University Ph.D. Thesis, 1966); J. Arpan, *International Intracorporate Pricing: Non-American Systems and Views* (Praeger, 1972); and J. Green and M. Duer, *Intercompany Transactions in the Multinational Firm* (Conference Board, 1970).

[7]For more elaboration, see J. Arpan's *International Intracorporate Pricing*, op cit.; and "Multinational Firm Pricing in International Markets," *Sloan Management Review*, Winter 1972–1973.

Such government policies obviously pose an accounting problem for MNEs who are *legitimately* allocating expenses to subsidiaries. For example, a U.S. firm bringing a Brazilian manager to the United States for training wants to charge the Brazilian affiliate for the expenses. But the Brazilian government says the subsidiary cannot pay the U.S. parent. What happens to the expense, then? It cannot be paid, nor can it be even "booked" in the Brazilian subsidiary's financial and tax records; yet the expense *has* been incurred. The usual answer or practice is for the parent company to enter the expense on *its* records for the Brazilian subsidiary, so that from an internal managerial viewpoint, the true expenses of the Brazilian subsidiary are known. However, the U.S. government does not allow this "expense" to be deducted for U.S. tax purposes, so the parent company ultimately ends up bearing the loss.

Setting Transfer Prices

How then do accountants set transfer prices? There are two general approaches, one based on costs and the other on market prices. For products, cost-based systems begin with an internal measure of production costs (standard costs, variable costs, total costs, and so on) then typically add a reasonable profit margin to arrive at the final transfer price and to allow a profit to the selling unit—for example, full cost plus 15%. The market price method uses as a valuation basis the price at which the product is generally sold to unaffiliated buyers, but may also include a percentage *reduction* in the market price for services performed by the buying unit (generally not performed by unaffiliated customers) simply to allow the buying unit a greater margin of profitability.

Clearly, the two methods converge toward the same price as the "plus" in the "cost plus" method increases and the "minus" in the "market price minus" method increases. For example, cost plus 50% equals market price minus 25% for a product with a cost of $50 and a market price of $100. Therefore, the choice of the particular method used depends on several non-price (that is, non-cost) factors. Accountants typically prefer cost-based methods because costs are generally more readily available, determinable, and verifiable, and because it is often difficult to determine an accurate "market price" (particularly if the product or service transferred is not sold to any unaffiliated customer). Cost-based methods are also more flexible because the specific elements that enter into the determination of the product cost as well as the profit margin (the "plus" in the transfer price) can be easily altered. On the other hand, most governments prefer market-based methods because they are generally less subject to manipulation by MNEs, and are more easy to assess in terms of "fairness." Finally, performance evaluation is more straightforward if market-based transfer prices are used.

Generally, the final determination of transfer pricing methods, and the actual prices, ultimately rests on the overall global considerations of the MNE's headquarters staff, and increasingly on specific government rules for transfer pricing. For example, the United States government specifies the use of market-based transfer prices unless a firm can justify why cost-based transfer prices are more "fair" and reasonable than ones based on market prices.[8] These final decisions are generally made *not* by accountants but by the top financial officer of the parent company. However, accountants play an important role in providing cost and revenue data for the final decisions, and in estimating the financial impact of various alternative prices. They also spend many hours *eliminating* intercorporate profits during consolidation. That is, according to both U.S. GAAP and taxation rules, all intercorporate profits must be eliminated during the consolidation of financial and tax reports. The accountants for an MNE who must perform these eliminations have no easy task when there are thousands of intercorporate transfers taking place annually among a hundred units in as many countries, most of the time at different values.

CONTROL

Earlier in this chapter, we pointed out that planning, while being for an MNE more difficult than for a domestic company, is also more critical for an MNE. The same is true for control, and essentially for the same reasons. Because operations are more likely to get out of control for an MNE, control is more important for an MNE. There is also a definite relationship between planning and control. The planning process is a form of control, and controls should be part of the planning process. The control process seeks to enforce managerial compliance with the

[8]See Section 402 and 402(A) of the U.S. Tariff Act of 1930 as amended, and section 482 of the U.S. Internal Revenue Service Code (including the appended regulations that went into affect in April 1968).

plan, and also serves as an ongoing evaluation of the results of the planning process.

It should be recognized that the degree of control that is and can be exercised varies over time and with the complexity of a firm's operations. There is a general growth and loss of control as a firm grows in size and complexity.[9] That is, as a firm's operations become larger and more complex the need for more centralized control grows; but at some point, operations become too large and complex to manage with the same degree of centralized control, and at that point, control becomes more decentralized. Finally, it is not possible to control everything, and keep in mind that control is expensive. As a result, firms selectively control some areas more than others. Some aspects of business operations remain so critical for survival that centralized control over them is maintained no matter how large or complicated the firm becomes. This is especially true for the financial function.

The Control Process

The control process relies on many forms of written, verbal, and nonverbal communication, and on physical observation. Doing business in several countries at once makes all of these forms of control more difficult to maintain for reasons that by now are very familiar to the reader: problems of distance, changing environmental and competitive conditions, and cultural differences. One major aspect of control handled by accounting personnel, the audit, is described in the following chapter. This chapter will concern itself with the other "non-audit" aspects of control involving accountants. The two principal aspects are procedural methods and performance evaluation.

Control Procedures

One kind of control is preventive rather than diagnostic. That is, it seeks to prevent events from going awry or deviating from the plan. In this category of control are a host of policy and procedural statements and manuals—many of which pertain to accounting, either directly or indirectly.

Accounting procedural manuals are an illustrative example. They

[9]For a comprehensive discussion of these points, see S. Robbins and R. Stobaugh, *Money in the Multinational Enterprise: A Study in Financial Policy* (N.Y.: Basic Books, 1973).

typically enumerate accounting procedures to be followed by all operations to safeguard assets, to record and report accounting information (by whom, to whom, by what method, and under what circumstances), and so on. These matters must be communicated and adhered to by all units, regardless of what local laws and regulations require. Without these procedures, a U.S. MNE, for example, would never know exactly the state of its own affairs, and, in some cases, it might even find itself violating U.S. law.[10]

At first blush, such policy and procedural manuals may not seem difficult to prepare. But as usual, the international dimension finds several ways of complicating matters. First, someone must suitably translate the manuals into as many languages as the MNE operates in. Second, the policies and procedures must be flexible enough to accommodate differences in operating environments—for example, covering both entry and recording procedures for computerized and noncomputerized (manual) locations. And if any of the procedures are truly "foreign" to particular environments, they must be explained sufficiently to permit employees to learn them properly. For example, a simple reference to maintaining financial records in accordance with U.S. "Generally Accepted Accounting Principles" is likely to mean nothing to a Nigerian accountant working for the U.S. firm's affiliate in Lagos. Finally, control procedures may have to be more comprehensive and strict in some countries where graft and corruption are more common. Therefore, MNE control manuals must be carefully designed and oriented toward education and training.

Management Information Systems

A critical tool of control is the firm's internal management information system (MIS)—in a sense, the nervous system of the firm. Through the MIS, the brain (the headquarters) of the firm is connected to all of its functioning parts—transmitting and receiving thousands of bits of information every day—in order to learn whether corrective adjustments are necessary in the firm's operations. If the firm is to succeed, the MIS lines must be kept clear and operational with little extraneous noise.

Critical to a successful MIS is the uniformity of the information processed. That is, information must be uniformly prepared and collected

[10]For example, without a clear statement of policy and an internal control system, a U.S. MNE might find itself in violation of the U.S. Foreign Corrupt Practices Act, as described in more detail in Chapter 7.

if it is to be properly analyzed, easily aggregated, and readily disaggregated. Therefore, a common format, language, currency denomination, and set of procedures must be developed and followed. Otherwise, the MNE can become a tower of Babel with accounting information coming and going in different languages, currencies, formats, and governed by various underlying procedures. The accounting and reporting procedural manuals mentioned above play a key role in achieving this needed uniformity.

The amount of information processed each day by an MNE is truly awesome. For example, a study of Eastman Kodak revealed that some managers were recieving annually over 200 regular financial reports consisting of more than 1300 documents.[11] A study of another multinational showed over one hundred types of reports flowing into headquarters, *excluding* all basic financial statements and all budget and other reports prepared solely on the subsidiary levels, for a total of over 55,000 total reports processed at headquarters during a year's time.[12] The headquarters of one of the largest Japanese trading companies i said to process over 2,000 bits of new information *daily* in its interna tional MIS. Furthermore, as pointed out in Chapter 3, the information needs of MNEs have steadily increased over the past few years as ad ditional groups within and outside the firm have demanded more information, and as competitive conditions have increased. At the same time, though, there is always the danger of information overload. So the MIS must be designed to prepare, collect, analyze, store, and report only information that is essential for decision-making, control, and reporting purposes. As a result, the degree of uniformity in an MIS is tempered by both organizational requirements and operational characteristics.[13]

Organizational requirements refer to the degree of control desired. For example, higher degrees of control require more centralized and uniform systems, more types of information, and more frequent reporting. Lower degrees of desired control lessen these needs.

---

[11]A. F. Brueningsen, "Kodak's Financial Information and Reporting System," *Management Accounting*, September 1975.

[12]George Watt, Richard Hammer, and Marianne Burge, *Accounting for the Multinational Firm*, New York: Financial Executives Institute, 1977, p. 244.

[13]For more discussion of these points, see P. Bohos "Management Information Systems for International Operations," *The International Accountant*, January–March 1972, pp. 6–8; and P. Dickie and N. Arya "MIS and International Business," *Journal of Systems Management*, June 1970, pp. 8–12.

Operational characteristics refer to the maturity and stability of operations and environments, and the confidence of headquarters in affiliate management. The MIS requirements are fewer for a well-established operation in a stable environment managed by a seasoned group of executives. The requirements are higher, more extensive, and more frequently applied for an operation with the opposite characteristics. Therefore, while the MIS must be uniform in terms of its preparation and format, the number of items and the frequency of their transmission may and should vary from one affiliate to another.

Another MIS complication for a multinational surrounds the means of communication, that is, mail, telephone, telex, courier, and so on. The choice of the means is dictated by the urgency and cost of the transmittal, the degree of secrecy desired, the reliability of the method of transmittal, and in many cases, the availability of certain forms of transmittal. The mail system is generally the method costing the least but is one of the slowest methods, as well. In many countries, it is also often unreliable and subject to government "inspection." Telex service, and in some areas, even telephone service, is not always available. And in almost all cases, there is a need to code information for security reasons. Thus, the properly designed MIS must take all of these transmittal considerations into account.

A final complication of a multinational's MIS is the involved process of assuring that the needed information reaches only the appropriate personnel. The cost of sending information to the wrong people is high, just as high, in fact, as the cost of sending people the wrong information. In addition, it is not always desirable (and it is sometimes costly) for people in one foreign subsidiary to receive information that pertains to another. For example, employees in one country may demand benefits similar to those given their counterparts in another country if they learn of some different treatment through the firm's MIS, even though they may not be entitled to or deserving of those benefits. At the same time, they do need to be informed of events in other affiliates or countries that will have an impact on their operations. Thus, the MNE must make sure that the MIS provides all key personnel with the information they need, but not with information they do not need or should not have.

Performance Evaluation

The performance evaluation process serves several purposes. As part of the control system, it provides information on how operations are going, and/or how they went. Performance evaluation is an assessment of the effectiveness and efficiency of current strategies, plans, and activities, which tells the firm whether they need to be altered. By making employees aware that they, too, will be evaluated and on the basis of certain criteria, the firm through performance evaluation also attempts to motivate personnel and direct their behavior in certain desirable ways—the classic carrot and stick concept. Finally, performance evaluation plays a well-known role in the areas of promotion and financial remuneration. It identifies both good and bad performance, and as a result, shows who should be promoted or demoted, whose salary should be raised or cut, who should share in the profits and to what extent, and so forth.

While there is much to be considered in the proper design and use of a performance evaluation system, one thing is sure. If the system is inadequate, the firm will soon be in financial trouble. Operations will be seriously, if not irreversibly muddled before top management is even aware that problems exist; and good managers may become so frustrated that they quit, while poor managers may be rewarded when they do not deserve it—all of which can soon put the firm in a rather precarious position. Note, too, the importance of the MNE being able to properly distinguish a subsidiary's operating results from the performance of the subsidiary's managers. For example, the operating results may be poor, despite the good efforts of the local management; that is, the results would have been even worse if the management had not done so well. In this example, failure to separate the two performance evaluations could lead to firing a good manager. The reverse of this situation is also possible. The favorable operating performance of the subsidiary could mask a poor (or less than desirable) performance by its management; that is, the operating results would have been even better if there had been better management. Thus, performance evaluation procedures must be designed to separate, to the extent possible, subsidiary performance from management performance.

In terms of the reward system, the key to the continuing success of performance evaluation is to properly reward desired behavior. That is, if corporate objectives are achieved as planned, and if the manager and the employees do what they were expected to do, then their behavior should be rewarded in some way. This is a clear signal to them that their behavior was consistent with corporate objectives, and a signal to all personnel that good performance is both desired and rewarded. The reverse is also true and equally important. Poor performance should be discouraged through the use of disincentives.

But a critical corollary to the entire performance evaluation process is to judge performance only in terms of what was controllable by the person being evaluated. That is, it is neither fair nor wise to evaluate negatively (or to punish) a manager whose performance was affected adversely by events beyond his or her control. Nor is it wise or fair to evaluate favorably (or to reward) a person whose favorable performance was due to luck or to other events outside his or her control. Therefore, a properly designed performance evaluation system must cancel out the impact of all the "uncontrollable" factors that resulted in a particular level of performance.

For example, consider the performance evaluation of a subsidiary manager in a country troubled by highly unstable economic and political conditions. Halfway through the year, a political coup occurs, a period of civil war ensues, all transportation and communication services are temporarily interrupted, all international transactions are halted, and the foreign exchange value of the currency falls by 50%. As a result, the subsidiary falls far short of the firm's sales and profits targets, and the translated value of the subsidiary's profits also declines. Yet despite all this turmoil, the subsidiary manager is able to increase the firm's relative market share in the country and keeps the subsidiary solvent. Should the subsidiary manager's performance be evaluated favorably or unfavorably? In terms of meeting the planned targets, he did not perform well, yet the reasons for that were beyond his control. In addition, he did perform well considering the highly adverse conditions encountered during the course of the year.

The example above illustrates some of the major complexities of performance evaluation within an MNE: myriad differences and changes in economic and political conditions, exchange rates, and currency controls.[14] These factors clearly make it more difficult to evaluate performance. Even greater difficulties arise when an effort is made to compare the performance of subsidiaries or subsidiary managements in different countries.

---

[14]For more information about these complexities, see J. Muriel, "Evaluation and Control of Overseas Operations," *Management Accounting*, May 1969, pp. 35–38; S. Farag, "The Problems of Performance Evaluation in the Multinational Firm," *International Journal of Accounting*, Fall 1974, pp. 45–54; S. Robbins and R. Stobaugh, "The Bent Measuring Stick for Foreign Operations," *Harvard Business Review*, September/October 1973, pp. 80–88; and H. Morsicato Gernon, *Currency Translation and Performance Evaluation in Multinationals*, (Ann Arbor: UMI Research Press, 1980).

First, the objectives for each subsidiary are often different, making it difficult to use a single method (or basis) for performance evaluation. For example, "increase in market share" may be an appropriate method for evaluating a sales subsidiary, but an inappropriate method for a manufacturing subsidiary with no sales force of its own. Or, for tax purposes, it may be desirable for the MNE as a whole to have a subsidiary in a country with a high rate of taxation show a loss, and another subsidiary in a country with a low tax rate show a profit. Using any method of performance evaluation based on "profitability" for *both* subsidiaries obviously would be inappropriate and unwise.

Second, the numerous differences in operating environments, mentioned earlier, also cause major problems in comparing the performance of subsidiaries in different countries. A manager in a stable environment has an easier task than one in a volatile environment. Or, if the foreign exchange value of one country's currency goes up and that of another country goes down, the translated dollar results of each operation will move in opposite directions, even though the local currency profitabilities of the two subsidiaries were the same.

So how well do MNEs do in resolving these problems of performance evaluation? Unfortunately, not always very well. While there is some recent tendency to use multiple and more sophisticated methods, several studies have shown that MNEs typically rely heavily on a single basis of performance evaluation—typically, return on investment measured in the currency of the parent company's country.[15]

What should they be doing? Optimally, they should be evaluating performance against the specific targets given to, and the objectives set for, each subsidiary, and even then, only on results that were within the control of subsidiary managers. An example will illustrate how this could (and should) be done.

Suppose a subsidiary imports some raw material from a subsidiary located in one country and then manufactures parts for a product which is later assembled by a third subsidiary in still another country. The manufacturing subsidiary's role is to produce the parts at a specific cost and level of quality, and deliver them on schedule at a certain import price to the assembling subsidiary. Changes in the exchange rates or customs duties will have an effect on both the importing subsidiary's and the manufacturing subsidiary's costs and revenues. Proper planning

[15]See J. McInnes, "Financial Control Systems for Multinational Operations," *Journal of International Business Studies*, Fall 1971, pp. 11–28; and H. Morsicato Gernon, ibid.

will predict such changes in terms of their direction, magnitude, and timing, and budgets and expectations will be set accordingly. But at performance evaluation time, the actual results should be compared to the planned results, taking into consideration what the exchange rates and customs duties actually *were* as compared to their projected levels used in the plan. Actual results can be recast using the planned rates, or the original plan can be recast using the actual rates. Either way shows the impact of the changes in exchange rates and customs duties over which the managers had no control, and which therefore should not be counted for or against the managers' performance. The parts manufacturing subsidiary can then be judged on the extent to which quality and shipment targets were met, and its managers in terms of the costs and revenues over which they had control (*after* the effects of the changes in exchange rates and customs duties are adjusted for). The performance of the assembling subsidiary can be judged in a similar way. And if its performance was affected by the poor quality or late shipment of the parts supplied by the manufacturing subsidiary, these adverse effects should also not be charged against the performance of the assembly operation's management, and so on.

In sum, an MNE must develop a fairly complex system of performance evaluation, taking into account differences in subsidiarys' objectives and operating environments, and in the degrees of control managers can exercise. While such a system is more difficult and costly both to develop and to operate, a simplistic one is likely to be misleading and, in the long run, potentially more costly, because without adequate performance evaluation the firm really doesn't know how well it is doing, or who is doing a good job and who is not.

ORGANIZING

The preceding sections of this chapter have enumerated several major complexities in managerial accounting for an MNE. They have also described an MNE's greater need for managerial accounting. As MNEs are faced with greater managerial accounting needs and complexities, it should come as no surprise that their management accounting areas must be thoroughly and appropriately organized. It also will come as no shock that *organizing* the management accounting area within an MNE is more complicated than organizing a domestic company's managerial accounting.

The assignment of responsibilities and activities for the firm's management accounting area is the first thing to be considered. As in domestic companies, in MNEs the primary responsibilities rest with the comptroller in corporate headquarters, with lesser, supportive responsibilities flowing down the corporate hierarchy to divisional comptrollers and ultimately to subsidiary comptrollers. Each comptroller on each level, in turn, assigns responsibilities to the individual members of his or her own staff. There is also an important interaction between the comptroller's organization and operations and those of the treasurer's, particularly as the former provides accounting and economic data to the latter.

Obviously for an MNE the sheer number of levels and people involved in these areas complicates matters. MNEs tend to be larger than domestic firms, have considerably more levels of management, and of course operate in more countries and diverse operating environments. Therefore, the assignment of responsibilities is more complicated. For example, how much and what kind of responsibility should be given to the comptroller of a Brazilian subsidiary manufacturing automotive accessories if the MNE is organized both by geographic area and by product division? The Brazilian operation is a part of, and hence responsible to, the Latin American area manager, but also to the automotive parts division manager, and to the parent company's headquarters, as well. If left entirely to his or her own devices, the Brazilian subsidiary's comptroller may develop or follow management accounting procedures and activities inconsistent with those in other subsidiaries, with obvious and potentially harmful or misleading results to the MNE as a whole. Therefore, the assignment of managerial accounting responsibilities throughout the MNE must reflect the needs of the MNE as a whole and be consistent with, and appropriate for, its organizational structure.[16]

A second major organizing problem concerns the capabilities of the firm's accounting personnel. Recall that accountants in all countries are not equally trained or skilled. And as we have pointed out several times, accounting for international operations requires skills greater than those required for purely domestic operations. Therefore, an important aspect of organizing the accounting area is developing the necessary skills of accounting personnel. This process entails more than just developing

[16]For a more detailed discussion of the organizational structure's interface with the control and MIS functions, see J. Arpan and L. Radebaugh, *International Accounting and the Multinational Enterprise* (N.Y.: John Wiley & Sons, 1981), Chapter 10.

a minimally acceptable (or uniform) level of basic accounting skills. It also requires the development of some skills specific to international accounting, such as currency conversion and the restatement of financial reports based on one country's procedures using another country's procedures. At certain levels, some nonaccounting skills must be developed, such as a capability in foreign languages—otherwise accountants in different countries of the firm's operations won't even be able to talk to each other! Thus, a considerable amount of personnel training must be done by an MNE before the organization of its management accounting area can be effective and efficient.

One other item to be considered in organizing the management accounting area is the internal management information system (MIS), described in the "Control" section above. The MIS must be organized consistently with the general organizational structures of the management accounting area, and the worldwide accounting staff must be properly trained to use it.

SUMMARY

Virtually every aspect and activity of managerial accounting is more complex in an MNE than in a domestic firm. Therefore, the design, organization, and implementation of the management accounting system must be very carefully considered. In addition, considerable effort must be made in terms of personnel training—otherwise the system will not work effectively or efficiently. Inadequate consideration given to any of these areas can prove, and will most likely prove, to be disastrous to the MNE's profitability, and ultimately, to its survival.

STUDY QUESTIONS FOR CHAPTER 6

1. How and why is the planning process more complicated for an MNE?
2. In preparing a present value analysis for a proposed investment in a foreign country, what kinds of complexities do MNE accountants face that they wouldn't normally face for a similar analysis of a domestic investment?
3. How do exchange rates complicate the budgeting process for multinational operations?

4. How and when do exchange rates complicate product costing for an MNE?
5. Other than changes in exchange rates, what factors make product costing more complicated for an MNE?
6. What are the two major approaches in setting transfer prices, and the advantages and disadvantages of each?
7. Why is there such international controversy over transfer pricing in international business?
8. Why is it that MNEs have greater control problems than domestic firms do?
9. What are some of the major ways MNEs attempt to keep things under control? What is the accountant's role in this process?
10. How do exchange rates complicate performance evaluation techniques for a foreign subsidiary?
11. Other than changes in exchange rates, what other factors make performance evaluation of a foreign subsidiary more complicated? Discuss the problems involved in comparing two subsidiaries to each other.
12. What can and should an MNE do to evaluate fairly the managers of foreign subsidiaries?
13. Why do the reporting needs of an MNE require such a complex management and financial information system?
14. What factors need to be considered in the design and operation of an MIS for an MNE?

ADDITIONAL REFERENCES

1. AlHashim, Dhia. "Internal Performance Evaluation in American Multinational Enterprises." *Management International Review*, Third Quarter, 1980, pp. 33–39.
2. Bursk, Edward C., et al. *Financial Control of Multinational Corporations*. New York: Financial Executives Research Foundation, 1971.
3. Choi, Frederick D. S. "Multinational Challenges for Managerial Accountants." *Journal of Contemporary Business*, Autumn 1975, pp. 51–68.
4. Choi, Frederick D. S. and Mueller, Gerhard G. *An Introduction to Multinational Accounting*. Englewood Cliffs, N.J.: Prentice-Hall, 1978, Chapter 8.

5. Duerr, Michael G. and Roach, John M. *Organization and Control of International Operations.* New York: Conference Board, 1973.

6. Fantl, Irvin L. "Control and the Internal Audit in the Multinational Firm." *International Journal of Accounting*, Fall 1975, pp. 57–65.

7. Farag, Shawki M. "The Problem of Performance Evaluation in International Accounting." *International Journal of Accounting*, Fall 1974, pp. 45–54.

8. Gorab, Robert S. "Effective Management Controls and Reporting Policies for the Multinational Company." *Selected Papers 1970*, Haskins & Sells, pp. 399–400.

9. Hawkins, David F. "Controlling Foreign Operations." *Financial Executive*, February 1965, pp. 25–56.

10. Knortz, Herbert C. "Controllership in International Corporations." *Financial Executive*, June 1969, pp. 54–60.

11. Mauriel, John J. "Evaluation and Control of Overseas Operations." *Management Accounting* (U.S.), May 1969, pp. 35–38.

12. Moore, Russell M. and Scott, George M., eds. *Introduction to Financial Control and Reporting in Multinational Enterprises.* Austin: University of Texas Press, 1973, pp. 52–57.

13. National Association of Accountants, *Management Accounting for Multinational Corporations*, Vols. I and II. New York: NAA, 1974.

14. Ricks, David A. *International Dimensions of Corporate Finance.* Englewood Cliffs, N.J.: Prentice-Hall, 1978, pp. 57–70.

15. Rueschhoff, Norlin G. *International Accounting and Financial Reporting.* New York: Praeger, 1976.

16. Scott, George M. "Financial Control in Multinational Enterprise—The New Challenge to Accountants." *International Journal of Accounting*, Spring 1972, pp. 55–68.

17. Scott, George M. "Information Systems and Coordination in Multinational Enterprises." *International Journal of Accounting Education and Research*, February 1974, p. 87.

18. Watt, George C., Hammer, Richard M., and Burge, Marianne. *Accounting for the Multinational Corporation.* New York: Financial Executives Research Foundation, 1977.

19. White, John D. "Multinationals in Latin America: An Accent on Control." *Management Accounting*, February 1977, pp. 49–51.

20. Woo, John C. H. "Management Control Systems for International Operations." *Tempo* Summer/Fall 1970, (Touche Ross), p. 39.

Chapter 7

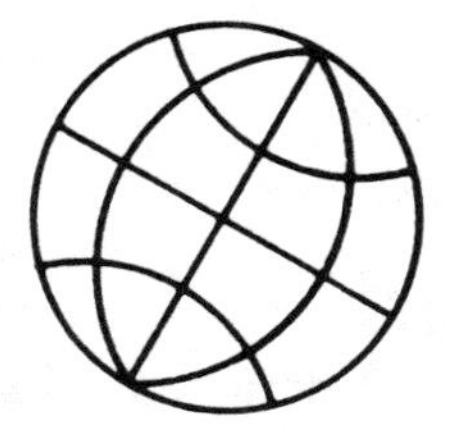

Auditing

In a general sense, auditing is done for the same purposes in all countries. Internal audits are done to see whether management's operating and financial controls are being followed, and whether or not they are effective. External audits are done to ascertain the validity and reliability of the financial statements prepared by companies, based on specific auditing standards.

Yet despite these general similarities, actual auditing practices vary considerably from country to country. In some countries an audit is seldom performed, or it is performed in a manner that is unacceptable to the auditors of other countries. Such differences in auditing practices pose problems for international investors and creditors and, of course, for multinational firms.

Here we will examine some of the major differences in auditing throughout the world, the problems these differences pose, and the steps being taken to mitigate those problems. The first part of this chapter is concerned with internal auditing, the second part with external auditing, and third part with some aspects of the international harmonization of auditing standards.

SOURCE: In this chapter, some of the material concerning professional auditing requirements has been abridged and adapted, with permission, from Touche Ross International's *Business Studies* series.

INTERNAL AUDITING

A good manager wants to be sure that the company's assets are used properly and safeguarded at all levels. Management also wants to be sure that employees behave in a manner consistent with corporate policy, and that they follow corporate procedures correctly. These two areas—asset security and personnel compliance—are the two key concerns of internal auditing. Without adequate internal accounting, firms can suffer losses due to the theft of products or funds or the misuse of funds or equipment. The firm can also face litigation if its personnel fail to follow company policy. Thus, internal auditing is an important function of management. Depending on the cultural and business practices of a country, internal auditing may even be one of the most important internal functions of a business.

Organization

Large corporations typically have a formalized internal audit organization and staff, the head of which reports directly to the executive management team or to the Board of Directors. Naturally, the size of the internal audit staff and the extent of their qualifications and training vary directly with the size and complexity of the company's operations. For a large multinational enterprise, it is not uncommon to find over a hundred people on the internal audit staff, with many of them residing outside the company's home country. At the other extreme, small domestic companies may not have any formal internal auditing organization or staff at all. These companies either do their internal auditing on an ad hoc basis, or rely on external auditors to make sure the operations are under control. For U.S. companies that operate internationally, however, informal or solely external forms of auditing are unacceptable. In fact, U.S. MNEs *by law* must have a formal internal audit organization and staff (see the discussion of the Foreign Corrupt Practices Act on p. 188).

Generally, most firms in developing countries are less likely to have formalized, sophisticated systems of internal auditing, if they have any at all. There are three main reasons for this: the personnel and operating costs of auditing systems are high; there is a general weakness in the auditing skills of their personnel; and there is a basic lack of awareness of how important internal auditing really is. Still, the awareness of its importance has increased, and firms have started to realize that the costs of *not* doing adequate internal auditing are high. So they have started spending the time and effort to hire or train the personnel necessary to develop and implement internal auditing systems.

The same trend is evident in large U.S. MNEs with respect to their *international* operations. The Foreign Corrupt Practices Act has forced them to develop or increase the size of their internal audit staffs, to develop new audit guidelines, and to hire or train audit personnel with international skills.

Problems in Internal Auditing on an International Scale

Geographic distance poses one of the most obvious problems in conducting internal audits on an international scale. The visual inspection of inventories becomes an awful task when the inventories are located on five continents, in a hundred countries, and in remote areas in many of those countries. The time, physical effort, and financial costs involved are substantial, to put it mildly.

Communication across great distances is another major problem. As we mentioned in the last chapter, in many countries the postal system is slow and unreliable: letters of confirmation may never reach their destination, or, if they do, they may never get back to the auditor at all (or they may take an excruciatingly long time to go in either direction). A nation's telephone service may also pose similar problems, although usually less severe. For example, some people, and even some companies, may not have phones (either because they do not want them or cannot get them). In the major cities of some developing countries the wait for telephone installation can be months or even years, because of long waiting lists for telephone service hook-ups. In more remote areas, telephone service is often not available at all. Unless the company is large and its international communications are frequent, telex machines are not economical and so they too are not a communication option available for internal audits.

Recall that the world is not on the same time worldwide either. Time zones pose communication problems that are not negligible. 4:00 P.M. in New York City is 11:00 P.M. in London and 5:00 A.M. (the next day) in Tokyo, so making an "instant" communication from New York with the staff in London or Tokyo is impossible, even though it may be vital.

Clearly, geographic distance and its consequent problems for communications make international auditing more expensive and time consuming than domestic auditing.

Other problems in international auditing are *cultural*. The problem of language is first and foremost. Auditors must be able to speak and write to various people to request needed information. If these people do not speak the auditors' language, the auditors must speak their language. While using interpreters is an option, it is expensive and often imprecise: key points can be easily misinterpreted. Being able to *read* the language is also important for obvious reasons: accounting is a written language, and local records will be kept in the local language.

Cultural differences also have an impact on business practices, thereby causing misunderstandings. In some Asian countries such as Japan, for example, it is considered impolite to ask for proof of someone's statement or assertion. To do so implies that the person providing the information is dishonest or unscrupulous—a serious insult not to be taken lightly. Because U.S. auditing practices typically require such proof, a strained atmosphere can develop quickly during an audit that is conducted in such countries.

Another problem can arise in the context of some cultures if the auditor is a woman. In many countries, women do not have a widely accepted basis for authority in the business world. A female auditor in such a country is not as likely to be taken seriously or to be given much information, even if she is an employee of the company. The same kind of native cultural resistance can arise if the auditor is of some nationality that is disliked or not respected (for whatever reason) by the people being audited. Stereotyping by nationality does exist, and would diminish, for example, the effectiveness of a Chilean auditing in Argentina (or vice versa) and a Frenchman auditing in Germany (or vice versa).

There are also certain differences in business practices around the world which can and do complicate the audit function. To cite just a few examples, in some countries cancelled checks are not returned to the issuer, but become property of the bank. Thus, auditors cannot verify by visiting the company that a check has been paid. In some countries, invoices are bought or sold on black markets, making the verification of invoices a difficult task. In many countries, suppliers and customers commonly do not respond to auditors' inquiries about accounts and notes receivable and payable because they simply do not want "strangers" to know about their financial affairs, or because they are just unfamiliar with this confirmation practice.

As we would expect from our discussions in earlier chapters, still other auditing problems arise out of different *accounting* practices. As we know, in some countries accounting is still in a very rudimentary stage. "Aged" accounts receivable may be unheard of, making it difficult for an auditor to find out how efficiently collection policies are being followed. Or, asset valuation techniques may be so different that the auditor must restate the assets using other methods. In still other cases, "off-balance sheet" accounting is common, making it more difficult for an auditor to find out what's really going on.

Finally, there is what could be called a "discomfort" problem. If the auditor is *not* a native of the country where the audit takes place, the auditor's effectiveness can be diminished by physical and psychological discomforts (such as fatigue and strain). The wear and tear of travel, the unfamiliar foods, and the effort involved in coping with numerous cultural differences can lead to the rather natural desire to "get in and get out" as quickly as possible. But unfortunately the consequence is often a less-than-optimal job on the audit.

Indigenous Versus Traveling Auditors

Because of the many cultural problems mentioned above, and because of the high costs of travel, there are some advantages in using indigenous (that is, local) auditors in each country instead of having a "traveling" team. Indigenous auditors are more familiar with their country and its business and cultural practices, and they know how to get things done when it seems to outsiders that things cannot be done or will never get done. Thus, local auditors experience no "cultural discomfort"; and they also do not incur the sizable travel expenses that "traveling" auditors need.

So why do firms use traveling auditors then? There are several reasons. First, a local auditor in each country can be expensive when a firm has operations in sixty to a hundred countries (and often the firm has to train them). Second, comparability of audits is more difficult to obtain when more auditors are involved. Third, local auditors are often less demanding in dealing with their fellow countrymen than "outsiders" are likely to be. Finally, local auditors are likely to be less familiar with the policies, needs, and desires of corporate headquarters. Thus, local auditors are not an automatic panacea to the problems of international auditing. In some cases, they may even exacerbate the problem.

How does a firm decide which approach or what combination to use?

One way is to examine the characteristic structure of its operations. A good illustrative example is provided by Exhibit 7.1. By examining where the company fits into this exhibit, some general decisions can be made with regard to home-based traveling auditors, auditors as local national residents, or a third variety, expatriate resident auditors.[1]

The Foreign Corrupt Practices Act (FCPA)

The Foreign Corrupt Practices Act is a U.S. law demanding that special audit attention (both internal and external) be given to a business practice that exists in virtually all countries to some degree: influence peddling. While this practice goes by different names in different languages—"bribery" in English, "mordida" in Spanish, "baksheesh" in Arabic, "bustarella" in Italian—the intent is generally the same: that is, to offer money or some service in order to persuade someone to do something beneficial for the company that normally he or she would not do without such an offer. Bribes include paying someone money to have an item imported that is not supposed to be imported, or to have the company exempted from certain taxes, or to be awarded a contract that otherwise would be given to another company.

Here is the painful Catch-22 for U.S. MNEs. In some countries, such payments are considered just a "normal business practice" and one that is not only unavoidable but sometimes mandatory if a firm is to operate successfully. In fact, influence payments are even considered legal in some countries.[2] But in the U.S. they are *il*legal. The investigations triggered by Watergate made it clear that many U.S. corporations were making such payments in foreign countries, and the question of the day became: What should be done? The crux of the issue was: Whose laws and cultural practices should govern U.S. firms operating internationally? In 1977, the federal government's answer came in the form of the Foreign Corrupt Practices Act (FCPA). In brief, the FCPA makes

[1]An example of an expatriate resident auditor is a German national employed by a U.S. company who lives and does his audit work in Brazil. The use of these expatriates typically arises when they are the most qualified local person available, or when no one from the parent company's country shows an aptitude for or desires working in the foreign country.

[2]In Japan, for example, the term "bribery" refers only to money paid (or services rendered) to politicians; firms can make bribes legally to other firms and deduct the cost as a business expense!

it illegal for any U.S. firm (including both its affiliates and anyone acting on behalf of the firm) to bribe a foreign government official. Penalties include a fine of up to $1 million for a company, and up to $10,000 and five years in prison for an individual.

There are some obvious business implications of the FCPA for U.S. firms. Unfortunately, because no other country imposes similar restrictions on the *international* operations of its firms, U.S. firms now operate at a competitive disadvantage. Non-U.S. firms can bribe to be awarded a contract or to receive some other favorable treatment whereas U.S. firms cannot (unless they want to risk prosecution). Thus, in countries where bribery is a fact of life, U.S. firms may lose business or other competitive advantages. While the overall business implications of the FCPA are both interesting and controversial, still they lie beyond the immediate focus of this book.[3] What lies *within* this book's focus are the accounting implications of the FCPA.

Accounting Implications

During the U.S. investigations of foreign payments, it was discovered that some firms were falsifying records in order to disguise "improper" transactions. Some were also failing to disclose the real purpose of certain transactions, while others, in remarkable examples of off-balance sheet accounting, were simply not recording some transactions at all. Firms were improperly recording revenues and expenses in order to hide bribes; or they were reporting fictitious transactions. (For example, a lawyer could be paid for services he never rendered, and he could then give the money back to the company which would not record the transaction; the company would thereby have that amount available to use in making a bribe.) As an example of "off-balance sheet" accounting, consider Braniff Airways, which sold over 3600 tickets in Latin America for a total of $900,000, did not record the sales, kept the proceeds in a secret bank account, and used the funds to pay extra expenses and commissions to travel agents and tour promoters.[4]

The specific accounting implications of such activities were twofold.

[3]For a good discussion of the FCPA controversy, see H. Baruch, "The Foreign Corrupt Practices Act," *Harvard Business Review*, Jan./Feb., 1979, pp. 32–50.

[4]For elaboration on this and other examples, see L. Radebaugh, "International Corporate Bribery: A New Dimension in Accounting," in Lee K. Zimmerman (ed.), *The Multinational Corporation: Accounting and Social Implications* (Urbana, Ill.: University of Illinois Center for International Education and Research in Accounting, 1977).

EXHIBIT 7.1 *Decision Variables for Selecting Internal Auditors*

	Home-Based Auditor Visiting Other Countries	*Local National Resident Auditor*	*Expatriate Resident Auditor*
Initial investment per man	Language training: $1,200–$1,500 Air travel per nonpeak season trip: $600–$800	Six months investment in training Salary: $12,000–$15,000 Travel: $ 600–$ 800	Language training: $1,200–$1,500 Moving expenses: $6,000–$10,000
Single, small audit location	Generally, not economically sound in any case; it would be better to request a management letter from the outside auditors		
Several small audit locations within same country	Generally sound, provided return engagements are anticipated	Generally not sound unless growth expectations in the short run indicate that the investment is warranted	
Several small audit locations scattered over several countries	Generally not sound; too much investment in languages	Generally sound if growth expectations in medium-range future warrant it	Generally not sound; too much investment in languages
Single medium-size audit location	Generally sound for one man on an extended trip, provided return engagements are planned	Generally not sound unless growth expectations in the short run indicate that the investment is warranted	

Several medium-size audit locations within same country	Generally not sound; too much travel between countries with attendant weariness from travel through time zones or excessive investment in languages	Generally ideally suited to this type of setup	Generally ideally suited to this type of setup
Several medium-size audit locations scattered over several countries	Ditto	Ditto	Could be sound if not too many languages are involved; could also work well jointly with a foreign national
Several large audit locations within same country or scattered over several countries	Ditto	Ideal, provided not too many languages are involved	Ideal, provided not too many languages are involved

SOURCE: Lee D. Tooman, "Starting the Internal Audit of Foreign Operations," *Internal Auditor*, November–December 1975, p. 60.

First, under these circumstances, naturally, financial statements did not accurately reflect the real transactions, because books and records were not being kept properly. Therefore, the FCPA includes a record-keeping provision which insists that books, records, and accounts must be made and kept to accurately and fairly reflect, in reasonable detail, the firm's transactions and the dispositions of its assets. Second, either firms were encouraging corrupt practices or they had such poor control systems that they were unable to detect or stop such practices. Therefore, the FCPA also includes a provision on internal controls which specifically says that each firm must

> devise and maintain a system of internal accounting controls sufficient to provide reasonable assurances that (i) transactions are executed in accordance with management's general or specific authorization; (ii) transactions are recorded as necessary (1) to permit preparation of financial statements in conformity with generally accepted accounting principles or any other criteria applicable to such statements and (2) to maintain accountability for assets; (iii) access to assets is permitted only in accordance with management's general or specific authorization; and (iv) the recorded accountability for assets is compared with existing assets at reasonable intervals and appropriate action is taken with respect to any differences.[5]

In the simplest terms, the internal control provision is saying that the firm must have a good control system to prevent bribery, while the record-keeping provision says that *if* bribes are made they must be properly recorded and disclosed! Yet perhaps the most sweeping aspect of the FCPA's accounting regulation is its movement into an area where government legislation has never previously ventured. For the first time ever, firms and their executives can face civil and criminal prosecution if the company's books are not kept properly or if an adequate internal control system is not developed and implemented—*even if no foreign bribes have been made.* It has become necessary not only to avoid wrongdoing, but to avoid even giving the appearance of wrongdoing.

EXTERNAL AUDITING

One of the major activities of a public accountant (as opposed to a private accountant) is to conduct "external" audits, an activity often re-

[5]Public Law 95–213 §102, the Foreign Corrupt Practices Act of 1977.

ferred to as the "attest" function. The auditor examines both the financial statements of a firm and the supporting evidence, prepared by the management's internal accounting staff. The external auditor tests and checks the accounting system underlying the financial statements, using as his basis the accepted auditing standards of the country—established by either the accounting profession or the government (or both). The audit and the related auditor's "opinion" are important because they lend credibility to the firm's financial statements.

While the external audit's general objectives are fairly similar in all countries—to determine that financial statements have been properly prepared and are not misleading—the exact meaning of "properly prepared" is generally *not* the same from one country to the next.

In most countries where external audits are required, the external audit is a "statutory" audit. The purpose of the statutory audit is generally to verify that the accounting records and financial statements have been kept and prepared in accordance with the country's related accounting laws. This legal approach to auditing is consistent with the legal approach to accounting in general in countries where accounting rules are established by statute. But in most cases, this approach to auditing does *not* result in the kind of financial statements deemed desirable in the United States, statements that reflect fairly the financial position of the firm and the results of its operations. For example, compare a typical auditor's opinion from the U.S. to one from West Germany.

> We have examined the accompanying consolidated balance sheet of (*name of company*) at December 31, 1981 and December 31, 1982, and the related consolidated statements of income, retained earnings, capital surplus, changes in shares of capital stock, and changes in financial position for the years then ended. Our examinations were made in accordance with generally accepted auditing standards, and, accordingly, included such tests of the accounting records and such other auditing procedures as we considered necessary in the circumstances.
>
> In our opinion, the statements mentioned above present fairly the consolidated financial position of (*name of company*) at December 31, 1982 and December 31, 1981, and the consolidated results of operations and changes in financial position for the years then ended, in conformity with generally accepted accounting principles applied on a consistent basis during the period.
>
> Arthur Young & Company
> February 13, 1983

According to our audit, made in conformity with our professional standards, the consolidated financial statements and the related report of the Board of Management comply with German law.
Dusseldorf, April 22, 1983.

Treuarbeit
Aktiengesellschaft
Wirtschaftsprufungsgesellschaft
Steuerbertaungsgesellschaft

Dr. Jordan — ppa. Baumeister
Wirtschaftsprufer — Wirtschaftsprufer

In short, the U.S. opinion says that the statements "present fairly the financial position" of the company according to "generally accepted accounting principles." The German opinion merely says that the financial statements and the related management report "comply with German law." No mention is made of whether they "present fairly" the financial position of the firm.

This is not to suggest that one country's auditing practices or audit opinions are better or more accurate than another's. Both are acceptable and accurate within the legal, sociocultural, economic, and accounting environment from which they emerge. The major differences are a consequence of the related differences in the accounting rules, standards, and practices of each country, as we described them in Chapters 1 and 2. It is precisely these differences that make external international auditing so difficult. You cannot have each subsidiary audited by local auditors and end up with a complete picture of the multinational enterprise, because each local auditor will be using a different yardstick as his guideline.

Problems of Conducting International External Audits

Most if not all of the previously discussed problems surrounding the *internal* international audit equally hinder the *external* audit. In other words, the external auditor also faces problems caused by geographic distances and the differences in cultural, business, and accounting practices. But external auditors also face some additional problems.

First, their audit guidelines and practices are generally more strict than those of internal auditors, since their audit opinions carry more weight and have far greater legal implications and consequences than the opinions of internal auditors. Second, an external auditor must have more knowledge and skill than an internal auditor. That is, the external auditor must assess the adequacy of a firm's internal control system relative to other firms in similar operating conditions—which is not necessarily something that an internal auditor must do. In terms of skill, note that unlike the internal auditor the external auditor is an "outsider" and is therefore less likely to be given as complete information by employees or to be as aware of all of the operating nuances and complexities of the audited firm's activities. Finally, the external auditor must not only assess all the accounting documentation of a firm's financial statements, but also the accuracy and adequacy of the internal audit staff's work (and workings) as well. For auditors of U.S. firms, this assessment of internal controls has assumed more importance since the passage of the Foreign Corrupt Practices Act.

As a consequence of the problems listed above, the shortage of qualified *external* auditors is even greater than the shortage of qualified *internal* auditors—"qualified" in this sense meaning meeting certain ethical and professional standards of training and practice, particularly those of the United States and the United Kingdom.

As we mentioned in Chapter 1, American and British public accountants must pass extensive and rigorous certification exams in order to be qualified to conduct external audits. But this is not always the case for the public accountants of most other countries, and it is particularly not the case for the accountants of developing nations. Even accountants who are qualified to conduct statutory audits often do not meet the qualification standards necessary to conduct U.S.- or U.K.-style external audits. For example, in many countries the statutory auditor may be a shareholder of the company he is auditing, or he can have other financial interests in the company (for example, he could be a creditor). This is a clear violation of the U.S. "independence" requirement. Also in some countries, there are no special qualifications required of a statutory auditor in terms of experience, certification, or educational training.

A few other specific illustrative examples of the international differences in auditing practices will clarify the range of possibilities involved here.

1. In Italy, statutory audits are the only required form of audit. It has not been a common practice in Italy to engage the services of public accounting firms because there are no legal or commercial requirements to do so. Statutory auditors may have financial interests in the company they are auditing, although they cannot be a director or an employee of the company.

2. In Germany, among the major professional rules of auditing are in-

dependence, impartiality, concientiousness, responsibility, and confidentiality. There is also strict prohibition of promotional advertising, and the auditor cannot be an employee of the company or a member of the client's management or supervisory board or have any participation in management. However, some German banks own auditing firms that audit companies which the banks own shares of or extend credit to. A rather unusual aspect of the German audit is that the auditor's opinion covers the management report, which is a narrative accompanying the financial statements, in addition to the financial information in the statements themselves. They ensure that the narrative does not contain misleading statements.

3. In France, the professional rules and ethics are found in legal statutes and amendments, and are similar to those in countries with developed accounting professions. In France, the auditor's report itself is required to comment on the financial statements and on the financial information given in the director's report. It gives an opinion on the "regularity and sincerity" of the statements—terms which refer to the statements' conformity to the law (regularity) and the fairness of their presentation (sincerity).

Because of lack of detailed auditing, statutory auditors' reports are usually confined to stating that the financial statements are in accordance with legal requirements and corporate statutes. They are not required to disclose matters such as contingent liabilities and profit distribution restrictions. While the specific duties of statutory auditors are prescribed in the Civil Code, auditing procedures are not mentioned. Typically, the statutory auditors meet quarterly as required, examine cash and securities, and record the results of their examination in the minute book maintained for their meeting. It is *not* a common practice to review the system of internal control, to confirm bank balances or receivables and payables, to observe inventory, or to review post-balance sheet events.

4. In Spain, by law the accounts of all corporations or publicly held companies must be audited by shareholder auditors. However, these shareholder auditors need not have any particular professional qualification or experience. For these and other reasons too numerous to mention, the standards of statutory auditing are low. And even though the Spanish Stock Exchange rules require that any listed company must also appoint at least one independent auditor who is a member of the Professional Accountants' Institute, the Stock Exchange and the Institute disagree on the scope of the auditor's examination. Typically, Spanish auditors do not report on whether the accounts give a "true and fair view," nor do they comment on the consistency of the accounting principles followed.

5. In Colombia, the Superintendant of Companies (the head of a government agency) periodically issues rulings and regulations regarding accounting principles and the presentation of financial statements. However, no body of accounting principles that are generally accepted by the profession has ever

been compiled into one publication, and the individual statutory auditor often signs financial statements solely on the basis that they agree with the books of account! Thus, the audit performed by a statutory examiner is often directed toward merely checking the financial statements against the legal rules of bookkeeping, and so it cannot be considered a complete and comprehensive audit.

Given these and literally hundreds of other international differences in auditing practices and standards, how does a multinational firm obtain a consistent, comprehensive external audit of its operations? Only by having its audits done in a consistent manner and by using the same yardstick throughout. For a U.S. multinational enterprise, this means having all its affiliates (U.S. and non-U.S.) audited by qualified persons familiar with U.S. audit standards and practices and with U.S. generally accepted accounting principles. Furthermore, these people must also be familiar with the local accounting practices and the rules with which local books must be in accord. Yet for reasons that should be clear by now, this is not an easy task. Few public accounting firms have such internationally trained auditors. In fact, there are not many more than a dozen firms throughout the world that have the capability to conduct a global audit suitable for a truly large multinational. These international accounting firms deserve a closer look in our discussion.

The Structure and Operations of International Public Accounting Firms

No treatment of external auditing's international dimension would be complete without some discussion of the large international accounting firms.[6] The well-known ones are frequently referred to as "the Big Eight": Arthur Andersen; Arthur Young; Coopers and Lybrand; Deloitte Haskins and Sells; Ernst and Whinney; Peat, Marwick, Mitchell; Price Waterhouse; and Touche Ross. These firms have their own offices or representative offices in virtually every country, and offer a full range of international services: auditing, tax, management information systems, and management consulting. Through their own

---

[6]For more thorough coverage of international accounting firms, see D. Hackett and F. Wu, "The Internationalization of U.S. Public Accounting Firms," *The International Journal of Accounting*, Spring 1977, pp. 81–91; and L. Radebaugh, "A Multinational Partnership? The Public Accounting Firm," a paper presented at the Annual Meeting of the Academy of International Business, Dallas, Texas, December 1975.

staff, and through those of their representative firms, they have a considerable cadre of international accountants who are generally well equipped to handle the problems of performing an external audit internationally.

These large firms developed their international capabilities because they followed the international movements of their clients. As U.S. and European enterprises established foreign production facilities, their accounting firms had to offer the same services abroad that they were accustomed to offering only domestically. If a particular accounting firm wanted to service its client better or simply did not wish to lose its client to another firm that could offer such services abroad, it had to develop the newly desired international capabilities.

First the larger accounting firms themselves opened and began operating branch offices in major foreign cities. During the 1970s, as competition significantly increased, there also occurred a rash of mergers and acquisitions, particularly in Europe. And in several foreign countries (especially in Latin America) where these accounting firms were legally forced out by waves of nationalistic legislation, the firms reestablished their presence by means of representative or correspondent offices with locally owned accounting firms.[7]

When international expansions are done by way of correspondent or representative relationships, the partners in other countries remain separate, autonomous organizations. Instead, the domestic and foreign firms are linked together by mutually beneficial services (rather than by equity or ownership relations), and by a common code of ethics and practice guidelines. In other words, each can perform services for the other in a manner that both find mutually reliable.

In order to better integrate worldwide operations, some of these firms have organized worldwide partnerships. By doing so, better cooperation is developed even though each individual partnership maintains a separate identity. According to Ernst and Whinney, it created Ernst and Whinney International in 1979 in order to have "an increased ability to maintain uniformly high quality standards around the world; a better coordination of investment in research, communications, and professional development; and a more effective management of human resources."[8]

---

[7]However, some firms established representative offices as early as the early 1900s in Europe.

[8]From a pamphlet by Ernst & Whinney in 1979 announcing the change.

Smaller public accounting firms have also become involved in international ventures. For example, there is a federation of thirty-six small- to medium-sized firms operating in thirty-nine countries. In this manner, the small individual firms seek to match collectively the international services offered by the Big Eight.

Yet all public accounting firms, regardless of their size or configuration, face a similar problem in operating internationally: developing and maintaining a uniform standard of practice and performance. The problem arises from the fact that accounting rules and practices continue to vary among countries, as well as the qualifications and skills of the auditors themselves. These problems will remain until international differences are eliminated, or at least considerably diminished, through the process of harmonization.

THE INTERNATIONAL HARMONIZATION OF AUDITING STANDARDS

Previous sections of this chapter have discussed two major points: first, there are considerable differences in the auditing practices and professions throughout the world; and second, these differences, combined with geographical, cultural, and business factors, make international auditing far more complicated, expensive, and difficult than domestic auditing is. In themselves, these problems might be enough to discourage even the hardiest of souls from pursuing a career in international auditing.

But on the bright side, many of these problems are diminishing. A number of international organizations are pursuing steps that are directed toward eliminating differences in auditing standards, practices, and practitioners. As described in Chapter 2, this general process is called harmonization. While it still has a long way to go, some progress has been made. Let us discuss, then, the major actors on behalf of harmonization, their activities, and what successes they have had to date in harmonizing the *audit* area.

The International Federation of Accountants (IFAC)

As was mentioned in Chapter 2, the IFAC is part of the International Congress of Accountants (ICA), an organization formed in 1904 with the major objective of increasing the interaction and the exchange of ideas between accountants of different countries. More specifically, the IFAC was established in 1977 to set international standards of auditing, ethics, education, and training. It also seeks the reciprocal recognition of qualifications to practice, and promotes the development of both regional accounting organizations and broad agreements on common aims for the accounting profession at large. The IFAC operates through five standing committees, all primarily concerned with auditing and accountants; there are committees on international auditing practices, education, ethics, financial and management accounting, and planning.

The objective of the IFAC's International Auditing Practices Committee is to develop guidelines on auditing and reporting practices and to promote the international acceptance of these guidelines. To date, it has issued twelve definitive International Auditing Guidelines, and it has Exposure Drafts outstanding on seven other areas related to auditing, as shown in Exhibit 7.2. The IFAC's Ethics Committee is currently investigating areas such as the advertising of and publicity for accountants; technical competence; and the integrity, objectivity, and independence of auditors. In 1980, it issued its first definitive standard, entitled "Guideline on Professional Ethics for the Accounting Profession." The IFAC's Education Committee is examining the prequalification education and training of auditors and various continuing education requirements.

The Accountants' International Study Group (AISG)

The AISG was one of the earliest groups to seek harmonization, although its geographic membership and focus were more limited than the IFAC's. The AISG concentrated on the accounting and auditing practices of the U.S., the U.K., and Canada. In the auditing area specifically, the AISG issued studies on "Auditing Approaches to Inventory" (1968), "Using Work of Another Auditor" (1969), "The Independence of Auditors" (1976), and "Audit Committees" (1976). Before disbanding, the AISG had completed a total of eighteen studies.

The International Accounting Standards Committee (IASC)

The workings of the IASC are similar in many ways to those of FASB in the United States: it conducts research studies, circulates exposure drafts, does interim studies, and issues standards. From its initial found-

EXHIBIT 7.2 *Adopted Standards and Exposure Drafts of the IFAC's International Auditing Practices Committee as of April 1982*

Definitive Standards

IAG-1	Objective and Scope of the Audit of Financial Statements
IAG-2	Audit Engagement Letters
IAG-3	Basic Principles Governing an Audit
IAG-4	Planning
IAG-5	Using the Work of an Other Auditor
IAG-6	Study and Evaluation of the Accounting System and Related Internal Control in Connection with an Audit
IAG-7	Control of the Quality of Audit Work
IAG-8	Audit Evidence
IAG-9	Documentation
IAG-10	Using the Work of an Internal Auditor
IAG-11	Fraud and Error
IAG-12	Analytical Review

Exposure Drafts Outstanding

E-13	The Auditor's Report on Financial Statements
E-14	Other Information in Documents Containing Audited Financial Statements
E-15	Auditing in an EDP Environment
E-16	Events After the Balance Sheet Date
E-17	Computer-Assisted Audit Techniques
E-18	Related Party Transactions
E-19	Using the Work of an Expert

ing membership in 1973 of nine countries, the IASC's membership has grown to include the organizations of fifty-three other countries (all of which are classified as associate members). However, unlike the IFAC, which focusses primarily on auditing and accountants, the IASC's main objective is to develop standards to be followed in the *presentation* of audited financial statements.

Other Multinational Organizations

As we mentioned in Chapter 2, the United Nations (UN), the Organization for Economic Cooperation and Development (OECD), the

European Economic Community (EEC), the Inter-American Accounting Association (IAA), the Conference of Asian and Pacific Accountants (CAPA), and the Union Européenne des Experts Comptables Economiques et Financiers (UEC) are other formalized, multinational groups that have been working toward accounting harmonization. Like the IASC, however, most of them have not focussed much of their effort specifically on auditing. Of these groups, the European-based ones have been the most successful—that is, the UEC and the EEC.

The UEC has a large permanent staff and a dozen standing committees, and it generates recommendations on accounting and auditing issues. It also publishes an auditing handbook, an international accounting dictionary, and an international journal.

The EEC has also made strides toward harmonization by proposing "Directives" on the presentation and content of financial (annual) reports, on the methods of valuation and consolidation used to generate them, and on their audit and publication. Thus far, however, few of these proposed Directives have actually been accepted, due to lingering disagreements among EEC member nations. The example most specifically related to the subject of this chapter is the EEC's proposed Directive No. 5, which concerns external audits and the structure and management of limited liability companies. However, this proposed Directive met with so many major disagreements among the EEC countries that it was ultimately withdrawn.

International Accounting Firms

Despite the efforts of all of the groups mentioned above towards achieving harmonization, the real harmonization of auditing practices has occurred primarily through the efforts of the large international accounting firms. Through international exchanges of personnel, international training programs, and joint audits, accountants in other countries learned the audit techniques of the U.S. and U.K. firms, and vice versa. The accountants in other countries learned because the audit of any multinational firm required the uniform use in all countries of a single auditing approach and set of auditing standards. Therefore, the international accounting firms had to train people in other countries who would be working with them on the audit "in the U.S. or U.K. manner." The reverse education took place as a byproduct. That is,

U.S. auditors in training non-U.S. auditors had to learn about non-U.S. approaches, standards, and practices.

The reason greater success in harmonization was achieved by the international accounting firms (as compared to the multination, formalized groups) is simple. The accounting firms did not seek the harmonization of national accounting laws or systems—only the harmonization of auditing practices and standards for their particular audits.

SUMMARY AND CONCLUSIONS

Conducting an international audit, whether internal or external, is clearly more complicated, expensive, and time consuming than a domestic audit. It also requires considerably more skill and ingenuity, for the audit practices that are easy to apply in one country are often not as easily applied (and are sometimes *impossible*) in the next. It should also be clear at this point that one should not assume that a financial statement from and audited in another country is entirely reliable. Due to differences in accounting systems, auditing standards and practices, and the backgrounds of the accountants and auditors themselves, an "audited financial statement" from one country is *not* the same as one from another country. Even though many groups have made, and are continuing to make, efforts toward eliminating these differences, any major successes in harmonization are still far from being achieved. Thus, continued caution and study must be exercised for some time to come.

STUDY QUESTIONS FOR CHAPTER 7

1. What are the two main purposes of auditing?
2. How does geographic distance affect international auditing?
3. How do cultural differences affect international auditing?
4. What are the main advantages and disadvantages of using traveling auditors rather than a number of local auditors?
5. What kind of standard audit techniques of the U.S. might be difficult to use in a developing nation?
6. Why are external auditing standards so different in various countries? What problems do these differences pose for the potential investor from another country?

7. Why are the backgrounds of the public (external) auditors so different in various countries? Give some examples.
8. Why has there been so little success in harmonizing worldwide auditing standards and practices?
9. Why have international accounting firms been more successful than multination organizations in achieving uniform audit practices?
10. What business and accounting practices led to the passage of the Foreign Corrupt Practices Act (FCPA)?
11. How has the FCPA changed internal and external auditing practices and standards?

ADDITIONAL REFERENCES

1. AICPA International Practice Executive Committee. *Professional Accounting in 30 Countries.* New York: AICPA, 1975.
2. Bradt, John D. "The Foreign Corrupt Practices Act and the Internal Auditor." *Internal Auditor,* August 1979, pp. 15–20.
3. Choi, Frederick D. S., and Mueller, Gerhard G. *An Introduction to Multinational Accounting.* Englewood Cliffs, N.J.: Prentice-Hall, 1978, Chapter 4.
4. Ernst & Whinney. *Worldwide Statutory Audit and Reporting Requirements.* New York: Ernst & Whinney, Inc., 1979.
5. Lee, Marikay. "The International Auditor." *Internal Auditor,* December 1978, pp. 43–47.
6. Light, Walter F. "The Internal Auditor's Job as Seen by a Multinational Company President." *Internal Auditor,* June 1976, pp. 29–34.
7. Loftus, Joseph X. "Putting the Brakes on Foreign Audit Fees." *Price Waterhouse Review,* 21, 3 (1976), pp. 16–19.
8. Mann, Richard W. and Redmayne, Derek H. "Internal Auditing in an International Environment." *Internal Auditor,* October 1979, pp. 49–54.
9. McKee, Thomas E. "Auditing Under the Foreign Corrupt Practices Act." *CPA Journal,* August 1979, pp. 31–35.
10. Pomeranz, Felix. "International Auditing Standards." *International Journal of Accounting,* Fall 1975, pp. 1–13.
11. Schwartz, Ivo. "Harmonisation of Accounting and Auditing in the European Community." *Accountant's Magazine* (Scotland), December 1977, pp. 508–510.

12. Stamp, Edward, and Moonitz, Maurice. *International Audit Standards*. London: Prentice-Hall International, 1978.

13. Tooman, Lee D. "Starting the Internal Audit of Foreign Operations." *Internal Auditor*, November/December 1975, pp. 56–62.

14. Weinstein, Arnold K., Corsini, Louis, and Pawliczek, Ronald. "The Big Eight in Europe." *International Journal of Accounting*, Spring 1978, pp. 57–71.

15. Wu, Frederick, and Hackett, Donald W. "The Internationalization of U.S. Public Accounting Firms." *International Journal of Accounting*, Spring 1977, pp. 81–91.

Epilogue

Ever since the development of the double-entry system in the fifteenth century, accounting has grown steadily more complicated as economic organizations and their kinds of activities have grown more diverse and intricate. The relatively recent rapid increases in the international flows of capital, products, and technologies, as well as the emergence of the multinational enterprise, have moved accounting toward a complexity unprecedented in its history. In addition, these recent developments have occurred so quickly that they have posed more problems for accounting than accountants have yet been able to resolve to everyone's satisfaction. For example, continuing controversy and dissatisfaction surround accounting for the gains and losses from foreign exchange rate fluctuations. Therefore, if at times it appeared that this book on the international dimensions of accounting left some questions unanswered, it is because some questions in the field still exist to which there are no definite answers.

To be sure, the proper interpretation of financial statements always requires some caution. Numbers, no matter how solid or real they appear on paper, in truth are far less concrete than we often would care to admit. As we have attempted to point out, the fluidity of numbers is particularly striking when those numbers are in the financial statements either of firms in other countries or of firms with extensive international operations. If the reader now firmly accepts this single point, the authors will believe themselves to have accomplished much. If our book has sparked in the mind of the reader more than a momentary and passing interest in the international aspects of accounting, then even more has been accomplished. And finally, if this small book inspires some of its readers to become actively involved in international accounting research or practice, then truly a major accomplishment has been achieved. Because international business will continue to grow in volume and complexity, there will be a parallel need for internationalized accountants to grow in number and sophistication. While there will always be many problems in the realm of international accounting, the problems are great opportunities for accountants with vision, imagination, and courage.

Index